TABLE OF CONTENTS

Chapter 5: Manorial records after 1540

ACKNOWLEDGEMENTS

The work owes much to Dr C.J. Kitching and others on the staff of the Historical Manuscripts Commission as well as to my own colleagues Dr C.W. Brooks and Professor W.R. Ward who read all or parts of the first draft; they drew my attention to a number of mistakes and made other valuable suggestions for additions and improvements. I am grateful too to the following for permission to reproduce the photographs of manuscripts: the Provost and Fellows of King's College, Cambridge (Plate 1), the Controller of H.M. Stationery Office (Plate 2, a Crown-copyright record), the County Archivist of Hampshire as Winchester Diocesan Record Officer (Plate 4), the Warden and Fellows of Merton College, Oxford, and the Secretary of the Historical Manuscripts Commission (Plate 5, previously reproduced in *Cuxham Man. Recs.*, Plate 2), the County Archivist of Devonshire (Plate 6), the President and Fellows of Queens' College, Cambridge (Plate 7), and the Yorkshire Archaeological Society (Plate 8). Mr A.S. Cook and Dr A.T. Thacker, successive editors of the Archives and the User series, as well as the Association's Editorial Committee, have been patient and forbearing in the face of delays in completing the typescript. Finally my wife has saved all readers of the book from many of the infelicities that appeared in its first draft.

P.D.A. Harvey

University of Durham
7th June 1984

LIST OF PLATES

LIST OF FIGURES

ABBREVIATIONS

Ag.H.R.	*Agricultural History Review*
Beauchamp Regs.	*Two Registers formerly belonging to the Family of Beauchamp of Hatch*, ed. H.C. Maxwell Lyte, Somerset Record Soc. xxxv (1920)
Bec Docs.	*Select Documents of the English Lands of the Abbey of Bec*, ed. Marjorie Chibnall, Camden Soc. 3rd Ser. lxxiii (1951)
B.L.	British Library, Reference Division
Bodl.	Bodleian Library, Oxford
Bolton Rentals	*Bolton Priory Rentals and Ministers' Accounts, 1473–1539*, ed. I. Kershaw, Yorkshire Archaeological Soc. Record Ser. cxxxii (1970)
Cambridge Fields	*The West Fields of Cambridge*, ed. Catherine P. Hall and J.R. Ravensdale, Cambridge Antiquarian Records Soc. iii (1976)
Cart. Mon. Ram.	*Cartularium Monasterii de Rameseia*, ed. W.H. Hart and P.A. Lyons, Rolls Ser. (3v., 1884–93)
Coke, *Copy-holder*	E. Coke, *The Compleate Copy-holder* (London, 1641)
Crondal Recs.	*A Collection of Records and Documents relating to the Hundred and Manor of Crondal*, ed. F.J. Baigent, Hampshire Record Soc. (1891)
Ct. Baron	*The Court Baron*, ed. F.W. Maitland and W.P. Baildon, Selden Soc. iv (1891)
Cuxham Man. Recs.	*Manorial Records of Cuxham, Oxfordshire, circa 1200–1359*, ed. P.D.A. Harvey, Historical Manuscripts Commission, Joint Publications, 23; Oxfordshire Record Soc. l (1976)
D. & C.	Muniments of the dean and chapter of . . .
Dom. St. Paul's	*The Domesday of St. Paul's of the Year MCCXXII*, ed. W.H. Hale, Camden Soc. [Old Ser.] lxix (1858)
E.H.R.	*English Historical Review*
Fisher, *Treatise*	R.B. Fisher, *A Practical Treatise on Copyhold Tenure* (London, 1794)
Hatfield Surv.	*Bishop Hatfield's Survey*, ed. W. Greenwell, Surtees Soc. xxxii (1857)
Hearnshaw, *Leet Jur.*	F.J.C. Hearnshaw, *Leet Jurisdiction in England especially as illustrated by the Records of the Court Leet of Southampton*, Southampton Record Soc. (1908)
Henley	*Walter of Henley and Other Treatises on Estate Management and Accounting*, ed. Dorothea Oschinsky (Oxford, 1971)
Hornsey Ct. Rolls	*Court Rolls of the Bishop of London's Manor of Hornsey 1603–1701*, ed. W.M. Marcham and F. Marcham (London, 1929)
Jacob, *Ct.-Keeper*	G. Jacob, *The Compleat Court-Keeper* (1st edn, London, 1713; 8th and last edn, London, 1819)
Levett, *Studies*	A. Elizabeth Levett, *Studies in Manorial History* (Oxford, 1938)
Local Maps	*Local Maps and Plans from Medieval England*, ed. R.A. Skelton and P.D.A. Harvey (Oxford, 1984)
Marcher Lordships	*The Marcher Lordships of South Wales 1415–1536: Select Documents*, ed. T.B. Pugh, Board of Celtic Studies, University of Wales, History and Law Ser. xx (Cardiff, 1963)
Mod. Ten. Cur.	*Modus Tenendi Cur' Baron' cum Visu Franci Plegii*, ed. C. Greenwood, Manorial Soc. ix (1915)

CHAPTER I

INTRODUCTION

The manor

The word 'manor' first appears in England soon after the Norman Conquest, when we find its Latin form *manerium* in Domesday Book and related records. From the start it had two distinct but closely related meanings. It could be the residence of someone who had a claim to belong to at least the middle range of the landholding classes. This was clearly its primary meaning: it derives from the Latin *manere*, to remain, and is related to the English *mansion*, the French *maison*. And it is a meaning that it has continued to bear from that day to this – when we speak today of a manor the picture that comes to mind is the large house of a well-to-do country gentleman. Over the centuries the word has moved up in the world, and when the middle ages spoke of a house as a manor the nearest modern equivalent would probably be a substantial farmhouse.[1]

But much more often in medieval England manor meant a single administrative unit of a landed estate, whether or not it contained a residence of the holder. Already in 1086 the instructions for collecting the information for Domesday Book assumed that the whole country was divided into territorial units called manors, each held of the king by one landlord, the lord of the manor. A very large estate (which would often be called an honour) might contain a hundred or more of these units; a small one might consist of a single manor. The compilers of Domesday Book had some difficulty in applying these instructions, and they classed as manors landed properties very varied in size, value and structure. In this they anticipated later usage. Some manors of medieval England comprised an entire village: the manor-house with its farm buildings would serve as the centre for the home farm (the manorial demesne), while the villagers would hold small amounts of land as subtenants, paying rents in labour, produce or cash. Elsewhere, a village might well be divided between several manors, like Cottenham in Cambridgeshire with its six manorial lords, or it might extend far beyond a single village, like the vast manor of Wakefield that stretched over more than 150 square miles of west Yorkshire. A manor might consist only of demesne lands without any local tenants; equally it might be entirely in the hands of tenants and have no demesne lands at all. It might consist of no more than a group of town houses like the bishop of Ely's manor of Holborn in London. All that these various properties had in common was that each was administered as a single unit in the landlord's estate organisation.

This still does not mean that we should envisage (as the Domesday instructions seem to have envisaged) the whole of medieval England divided into neat manorial units like the pieces of a jigsaw puzzle, just as it was divided into ecclesiastical parishes. Manors might overlap so that a single area lay within more than one manor. This came about through enfeoffments or grants at fee farm, varieties of what we might call permanent leasing in return for military service or for other rents and services, often more or less notional: a landlord might in this

[1] It could, however, be a town house – e.g. a grant, about 1230, of 'my *manerium* which is situated in St Mary's street at Bristol', between two specified holdings (*The Beaulieu Cartulary*, ed. S.F. Hockey, Southampton Records Ser. xvii (1974), p.30).

1

way effectively alienate a manor while still deriving from it a rent or judicial rights that would be administered through another unit of his estate – that is to say, as part of another manor that remained in his control. The process might occur more than once. Thus in Suffolk, in 1325, Sibton Abbey's lands at Falsham 'are held in chief (*i.e. directly*) of Sir William de Bovile and beyond that of William de Monte Caniso as of the manor of Edwardstone and beyond that of the earl of Cornwall as of the honour of Eye and beyond that of the lord king'.[2] Here, while it was the monks of Sibton who saw to the tilling of the land and who drew direct profit from the property it was still held to be part of (that is, it produced rights or rents that were administered through) an unnamed manor of Sir William de Bovile; this in turn was part of William de Monte Caniso's manor of Edwardstone, which was itself held from the honour of Eye, one of the large estates of the great earldom of Cornwall. Ultimately, as here, all land in medieval England was held of the king, but several levels of tenure (and thus several overlapping manors) might intervene between the Crown and the local manorial lord.

This structure of manors was far from unchanging. Until the statute of *Quia Emptores* in 1290 the chain of tenure from the king downwards could still be extended, so that property could pass to form a new manor, a new unit in its lord's estate, while still remaining at least nominally a manor in the estate of its former immediate lord. But even within a particular estate, reorganisation of one sort or another could lead to the reallocation of properties between manors or the creation of new ones. Thus at the beginning of the fourteenth century Battle Abbey in Sussex created the new manor of Marley by forming a new administrative unit from its demesne lands near Battle itself together with recently acquired lands in the hands of tenants.[3]

These then are the two meanings of the word manor that we find from 1086 onwards: a residence, and a unit of estate administration. Later – probably not until the fifteenth century – manor acquired a third meaning: a piece of landed property with tenants over whom the landlord exercised rights of jurisdiction in a private court. Manorial courts, we shall see, had been held long before this, but now they served to define the manor itself; as Chief Justice Sir Edward Coke put it in the early seventeenth century, 'a Court Baron . . . is the chiefe prop and Pillar of a Manor, which no sooner faileth but the Manor falleth to ground'.[4] If there was no court there was no manor, and the word moved from the vocabulary of estate management to become a technical legal term, a position it retained from the sixteenth century to the twentieth.

It is easy to see how the word came to change its meaning in this way, for the three meanings merge into each other. A residence of the landlord – or of his lessee or bailiff – would be an obvious centre for managing his local properties forming a unit of management not only for organising agriculture and collecting rents but also for administering whatever judicial rights the landlord claimed over his tenants. What we see, in fact, is not so much changes of meaning as changes of emphasis over the centuries, and it is often difficult to know which meaning of

    [2] *The Sibton Abbey Estates: Select Documents 1325–1509*, ed. A.H. Denney, Suffolk Records Soc. ii (1960), p.43.
    [3] Eleanor Searle, *Lordship and Community: Battle Abbey and Its Banlieu 1066–1538*, Pontifical Institute of Mediaeval Studies, Toronto, Studies and Texts, 26 (1974), p.268.
    [4] Coke, *Copy-Holder*, pp.56–7.

the word is uppermost in any particular instance. It is worth remembering this when we look at other problems of interpreting manorial records: many of them arise through just this sort of barely detectable shift in the meanings of words.

It is with the second and third meanings of the word manor that we are concerned when we come to define manorial records, and this change in meaning gives us an oddly bounded subject. First, looking at manors as the administrative units of a medieval landed estate, all documents produced in the course of its day-to-day management are called manorial records. Then, taking the manor as an area under the jurisdiction of a private court, manorial records are the writings produced by that court in conducting its business. So manorial records are any records of local estate management during the middle ages, and the records solely of the manorial court in later periods; here we have taken 1540 as the dividing line. This division may seem to have little to commend it, but it does at least broadly correspond to sixteenth-century changes in the methods of estate management, in the character of the records and in the legal standing of copyhold tenure.

When we look at medieval estate management in general we have to remember that manorial records, the records of local management, show us only one level of administration and that on a large estate there will have been other levels as well. Besides the manorial courts there might be an honour court for the free tenants of the whole estate. Besides the accounts of receipts and expenses on a single manor there would be the accounts of the receiver who collected cash from all the manors of the estate; indeed, on a very large estate there would be several receivers and, at the top of the financial hierarchy, a receiver-general who would himself render account of what they paid in to him. These higher levels of estate administration are obviously closely linked to the local administration – they all belong to a single organisation – and we shall look, though briefly, at the records they produced when we discuss the related records from the manorial level. But beyond this, any medieval estate, large or small, was only half of a single institution. It was, so to speak, the productive half – the half that produced the money and goods that supported the consuming or spending half, the household. This household might be a corporate one – a monastery or a college. It might be the single manor-house of a knight or other member of the lesser gentry. Or it might be the large itinerant household of a great lay magnate or bishop. There was great variety in the households of medieval England. But their relationship to their estates was always the same: it was the household that expended what the estate produced. Medieval households made records of their own, though their quantity was probably considerably less than the estate records and certainly far fewer have survived. Occasionally in the thirteenth and early fourteenth centuries we find financial records covering the manors of the estate and the departments of the household as well, but in general the two organisations were kept quite distinct and we shall not be looking here at any household records.

Estate management, 1086–1540
To understand the records of medieval estate management it is essential to know something of its pattern of development. First, however, it is worth digressing for a moment to look at another word which historians writing about medieval manors and estates often use, but use in confusingly different ways: the word demesne (Latin *dominicum*). It is not that it has more than one meaning: it is always land that is directly under the control of the landlord, without the

intervention of a middle (mesne) tenant. But its significance varies with the particular context. Sometimes it is used of those parts of an estate that have not been let out to military tenants in return for knight service – in other words the manors from which the landlord draws direct financial profit. Sometimes it is used of manors that the lord runs through his own officials as against those that are in the hands of lessees (a distinction we are about to look at more closely). And on the individual manor it is used of the home farm, the lands that are tilled by the lord himself (whether through his officials or through his lessees) as against those that are in the hands of permanent local tenants (it is in this sense that we have used the word already).

When a medieval landholder's estate was small and compact so that he could keep it under his own eye he might well run it entirely himself, supervising, or himself sharing in, the day-to-day work of as many employees as were called for – his life would be very much that of the farmer today. It might contain only demesne lands or it might include lands held by local tenants. Throughout the middle ages there were innumerable estates of this sort in England, and these estates might be referred to indifferently either as free holdings or as single manors, that is, until the word manor came to be restricted to those that had tenants and a manorial court. When we look at the manorial records of medieval England it is easy to envisage clearly defined levels of free landholding: first the large estate or honour, then the manor, and finally the holding of a local manorial tenant. Easy, but quite misleading. In practice there was no clear demarcation between the manorial free tenant, who might well have a considerable property, possibly made up of lands held from several different lords and possibly with tenants of his own, and the manorial lord whose manor might well include lands held of other landlords either on temporary lease or by permanent tenure. Very often indeed the same man was both a manorial lord and a manorial tenant. Rather than distinct levels of tenure we have to reckon with a great variety of types of property.

The only real distinction was one of size; and when an estate was too big for the landholder to run it entirely himself – when it comprised more than one or two manors – he had a choice between two methods of management. He could instal in each of its units, or manors, an employee who would act as a bailiff, who would run the property on behalf of its lord, acting simply as his agent in meeting its expenses and getting in its profits. Or he could let the manor to a lessee who would hand over each year a predetermined rent in money or produce but would keep any additional profit. It is this second method of leasing that has normally been the more usual in England (as in Europe generally) and this was how estates were being run at the time of the Domesday survey in 1086 and for most of the twelfth century. When a manor was leased in this way it was said to be at farm (*ad firmam*): the farm (*firma*) was not the property itself but the annual rent, and the lessee who paid it was known as the farmer (*firmarius*) – another pair of words that can be confusing, for modern writers on agrarian history (though not the medieval texts themselves) use them also in their modern meanings of any agricultural estate and any substantial agriculturist. A lease might be for a term of so many years, or for one or more lives, that is of the lessee and his heirs. Even in the eleventh and twelfth centuries we find some variations on straightforward leasing: on the estates of St Paul's Cathedral Willesden (Middlesex) was in 1086 leased not to a single farmer but to the local manorial tenants acting jointly, while from the late twelfth century onwards many of the cathedral's manors were being leased to its own canons who probably ran them by some form of subletting.[5]

Nevertheless, most of the manors that made up the more substantial estates seem to have been in the hands of individual local lessees both at the time of the Domesday survey and for the hundred years following. Normally the lessee will have lived in the manor-house that, with its adjacent farm buildings, formed the centre of the property. However, a different pattern was introduced on the estates of the Cistercians. The first Cistercian monastery in England was at Waverley (Surrey) and was founded in 1128; the order spread rapidly and by 1200 some fifty houses had been set up and endowed with very considerable properties. It was a rule of the order that its monks and lay brothers should work their lands themselves and should not simply live on the rents and services supplied by local tenants and lessees. To underline this distinction, the administrative unit on a Cistercian estate was called not a manor but a grange (*grangia*), a word meaning barn, showing that it was centred not on a residence, whether of lord or of lessee, but only on the buildings needed for agriculture.

Within a century this had become a distinction without a difference. The late twelfth century saw a movement away from leasing as the normal method of running a large estate. Instead, landlords adopted the alternative method of appointing to each manor an official who would be answerable for all its receipts, the system known to historians (again confusingly) as demesne farming. There are some signs of the change in the 1170s but it was only in the mid 1180s that it became a general trend. It seems to have proceeded steadily on lay, episcopal and monastic estates alike; by the 1220s demesne farming had become the norm on most large estates and it continued to predominate until the mid fourteenth century. There are various possible reasons for the change; it occurred only in England and represents a break with the normal practice throughout Europe. It had wider implications than might appear, for its effect was to give the lords of landed property a direct interest in exploiting it efficiently and profitably and thus in the techniques of management and agriculture. And for the historian it was a development of great importance for it was the demands of demesne farming that produced the most informative of medieval manorial records, records that tell us more of medieval agriculture in England than we know from any other part of Europe, more of English agriculture in the thirteenth and fourteenth centuries than we know of any other period before the late eighteenth century. On the other hand, although predominant, demesne farming never became universal in England; it was never applied to the estates of the Crown, for instance, and even in the thirteenth or fourteenth century it can have been seldom that a large estate had none at all of its manors leased out to local farmers.

When demesne farming first came in, landlords managed their properties by a system of elaborate supervision, so that each official was closely watched in all his doings by another official placed above him. Taking the place of the lessee on the individual manor was the reeve (*prepositus*) who was probably from the start, as he certainly was by the mid thirteenth century, an unfree tenant of the manor, chosen for the post by the lord or by his own fellow-tenants. Like the lessee, he would see to the tilling of the demesne lands and the care of the livestock, with the help of hired workers and of whatever labour services were due from the tenants; like the lessee, he would buy and sell livestock and corn to best advantage; but, unlike the lessee, he would give the landlord all the profit he

[5] R. Lennard, *Rural England 1086–1135* (Oxford, 1959), p.153; *Dom. St. Paul's*, pp.xli–xlii.

made, not just the predetermined farm. Above the reeve was a bailiff (*ballivus*)
set in charge of two or three manors, and in charge of the whole estate (or of a
substantial portion if it was a very large one) was the steward or seneschal
(*senescallus*) who would regularly tour the manors, inspect the bailiffs' and reeves'
conduct of affairs and hold the manorial courts. Above the steward were the
auditors who checked the officials' accounts, and the lord himself. This is the
form of organisation described in the mid-thirteenth-century treatise called the
Seneschaucy. In its detailed workings – the officials' titles and their exact spheres
of responsibility – there were differences between one estate and another, but the
principle of management by a hierarchy of supervisors seems to have been very
general.

The system did not last long. The exact course and chronology of change
differed from one estate to another but the trend is clear. The hierarchy of
supervisors dropped away: the bailiff with oversight of two or three manors
disappeared altogether, the steward lost his duties of general inspection and was
employed only to hold the manorial courts. There remained only the lord's
auditors and the official on the individual manor, who was given a fairly free hand
to act as he thought best in the lord's interests with minimal supervision; he was
subject only to searching financial scrutiny once or twice a year. It may have been
improved methods of accounting that made this change possible; it produced a
simpler, less cumbersome system of management, but one that left the lord very
much at the mercy of a clever or unscrupulous local official. This official, in
charge of a single manor, might be a reeve (*prepositus*), a local unfree tenant who
would receive no payment beyond the remission of the rent from his own
holding; he might be a bailiff (*ballivus*), a local free tenant or an outsider, paid a
regular stipend; or he might be called *serviens*, a word often translated as sergeant
but better perhaps as servant or official, who might be either a bailiff or a reeve.
The removal of supervisory bailiffs and stewards was only the start of a process
that by the early fourteenth century was putting more and more responsibility
into this local official's hands. The economic and agricultural initiative, taken
over by the landlord when demesne farming came in, was passing back to the
man on the spot – from the estate centre back to the individual manor. Before
long the local official was being required to answer only for a predetermined yield
from the corn he sowed: any extra that he succeeded in harvesting through good
luck or good management was his to keep. Again, parts of the livestock – the
dairy herd or the poultry – might be hired out to the local official by the year; he
would pay so much for each cow or each hen and would keep the milk or eggs for
himself.

All this had the effect of making the reeve or bailiff less of a local agent of the
landlord and more of a lessee, himself bearing the risk and taking the profit of
running the manor. Also in the first half of the fourteenth century parts of a
manor's demesne lands were often leased out to local tenants – at first small areas
for no more than a year or so, but later larger areas for longer periods. This can
all be seen as foreshadowing the return to the leasing of entire manors. This
occurred in a much slower, more piecemeal fashion than the adoption of demesne
farming. It began on some estates well before the middle of the fourteenth
century: at Norwich Cathedral Priory manors were being leased out in the 1330s,
when their profits from demesne farming started to decline.[6] The changes that

⁶ E. Stone, 'Profit-and-Loss Accountancy at Norwich Cathedral Priory', *T.R.H.S.* 5th Ser.
xii (1962), pp.43–6.

followed the Black Death of 1348–9 hastened the return to leasing, as the profit margin of agriculture was reduced and it became harder to find and to keep satisfactory local officials. By 1400 leasing was once more the usual method of running a substantial estate. But it was still far from universal. In the late 1430s Taunton Priory in Somerset had all its manors at farm;[7] on the other hand Tavistock Abbey in Devonshire was still running four of its manors through its own officials in 1497 – here, as often happened, it was properties close to the estate centre that were kept in hand as sources of supplies.[8] On the estates of an itinerant lay lord or bishop the manors where his principal residences stood might be among the last to be leased – thus the archbishops of Canterbury mostly kept Otford (Kent) in hand until 1444.[9] And just as the leasing of an entire manor might be preceded by hiring out some of its livestock, leasing parts of the demesne lands and so on, once the manor as a whole had been set to farm portions of the property might be kept in the lord's hands; thus the sheep and pasture rights were often excluded from the lease of a manor. There was great variety in the manorial leases of the fifteenth century and some variety too in the way estates were managed.

At the same time the predominance of leasing imposed a certain pattern of organisation. On very large estates it gave added importance to the lord's council, which decided the forms and terms of the leases. And whereas there was now no need for auditors to check the accounts of manorial officers, the treasurer or receiver to whom rents were paid became the more important in that the whole of the lord's receipts from the estate now passed through his hands – none came in the form of produce from demesne manors. On individual manors the rents of peasant tenants were sometimes included with the manorial lease: the lessee would collect and keep them for himself and the amount of his annual rent would take this into account. Often, however, the landlord continued to collect the local tenants' rents through a local official of his own, usually called the collector (*collector reddituum* or just *collector*). The lessee himself was of course normally called a farmer (*firmarius*) – it is because the leasing of lands has been so general since the fifteenth century that farmer has come to acquire its modern meaning – but occasionally we find him referred to, confusingly, as a reeve or bailiff. The local manorial courts were nearly always excluded from a lease; they were kept firmly in the lord's own hands, and the steward who held them continued as before, still bereft of any managerial responsibilities on the estate.

This then was the general pattern of estate organisation in the fifteenth century, and still in the early and mid sixteenth when the dissolution of the monasteries and other changes produced a revolution in the ownership of landed estates in England, and when common usage among historians starts to confine the term 'manorial records' specifically to the records of the manorial courts. The legal and tenurial developments reflected in these later court records will be considered when we look at them in detail; the general structure and organisation of landed estates is not essential background to these records as it is for the medieval manorial records. But any outline of estate organisation from the eleventh century to the sixteenth – even if much fuller than here – can only point to the general trends. Differences in the size and composition of the manors comprising the estates, differences in the size, traditions or policies of the estates

[7] B.L. Add. Rolls 16333, 25873.
[8] H.P.R. Finberg, *Tavistock Abbey* (Cambridge, 1951), pp.256–7.
[9] F.R.H.Du Boulay, *The Lordship of Canterbury* (London, 1966), pp.221, 239.

themselves all made for individuality and variety at every stage of development. As we shall see, manorial accounts of the demesne-farming period are extraordinarily uniform in form and in content; yet one seldom reads one without finding some interesting feature peculiar to the particular estate, the particular manor or the particular account. Indeed, although the general pattern of manorial records at any one period is remarkably consistent throughout the country, yet there was still room for a good deal of minor variation, and local exceptions can be found to almost every statement that will be made here about the particular types of record, both medieval and later.

Written records in medieval estate management

What part did written records play in this developing pattern of estate organisation? From the late thirteenth century onwards the answer is fairly clear: we can see how the various types of surviving record were drawn up and used, and they themselves refer to other more ephemeral records that have mostly failed to survive. But for earlier periods it is harder to determine the role of writing in manorial administration. Thus it is difficult to tell whether the first appearance of a particular type of record marks the introduction of a new administrative technique or merely the application of writing to what had long been done – or whether, indeed, all we are seeing is a pattern of accidental survival. It seems, though, as if written records were little used in estate management until the end of the twelfth century; then they start to appear on a larger number of estates and for a wider range of purposes, a trend that continued with increasing momentum until the 1270s produced a rapid expansion that made the written record a normal part of administration on every type of estate.

These written records fall into three main categories – surveys, financial accounts and records of manorial courts – and we shall look at each in turn. It is important to remember that these are records that were written for landlords and their officials and that they thus show us the economy and society of the medieval countryside from their particular viewpoint. Thus they tell us more about a manor's contacts with other manors on the same estate than with other neighbouring communities; more of the tenants' customary obligations to the lord of the manor than to each other; much of what happened in the manorial court but nothing of what happened in the parish church. This of course is because they were drawn up as business records concerned simply with the efficient management of the estate for its owner. That means, however, that they give us a very one-sided and limited view of many aspects of medieval life and we ignore their particular bias at our peril. Smallholding tenants conducted their affairs without written records beyond the evidences of title to their lands – nor do we have any written records produced for the medieval farmers, the manorial lessees. This produces another odd imbalance. It means that for the period of demesne farming our records are those of the entrepreneurs, those who were taking the initiative in exploiting the land and drawing maximum profits from the direct practice of agriculture; but once manors had mostly been leased out again these same records are those of landlords who played a passive part and who simply drew their income from rents. Initiative had passed elsewhere, to the non-record-producing lessees, but this did not mean that it had ceased, or that there was any less innovation or enterprise than there had been before, either on a particular manor or over an estate as a whole.

Nor are these the only risks of misinterpretation in using manorial records. As with any record source we must bear in mind the particular purpose for which they were drawn up – which quite certainly was not in order to provide future historians with information about the age that produced them. A great deal about the economy of the medieval landed estate was obvious to those who wrote and used these records but is not at all obvious to us, and, even more than most medieval records, we must be very wary of taking them at face value for they contain many traps. In examining each type of manorial record we shall look at some of these traps that we can guard against; but there must be others that historians have not yet detected. And there is one further general bias that we should bear in mind. We have manorial records from estates of every size and description; but a quite disproportionate number of those that survive, particularly of those that survive in complete series, come from very large estates and from ecclesiastical estates, especially those of Benedictine monasteries. This will be apparent when we look at the locations of surviving manorial records.

Where to find manorial records
In the middle ages ecclesiastical estates – of bishoprics, monasteries, colleges, hospitals – achieved far greater stability and continuity than the estates of lay lords, which were divided, recombined or extinguished altogether following deaths, forfeitures and other chances of family fortune. This stability extended to the estates' records, and where the institution has continued in existence in some form or other the entire medieval archive may have survived undisturbed to this day. The manorial records of – to take some notable examples – Westminster Abbey, the cathedral priories of Canterbury and Durham, Merton College at Oxford, and Winchester College are still preserved in the buildings that formed the centre of each of these medieval estates. In some cases the records remain in the possession of the medieval institution or its direct successor, but have been transferred physically to a recognised archive repository for safe keeping: those of the abbey and bishopric of Ely are in Cambridge University Library, those of St Paul's Cathedral in the Guildhall Library, London. The estate records of the medieval bishoprics have been slightly less fortunate than those of ecclesiastical corporations, but some large archives survive, such as those from the archbishopric of Canterbury at Lambeth Palace and from the bishopric of Winchester in the Hampshire Record Office.

Sometimes the estates, and the manorial records, of one institution passed intact into the hands of another. The records of God's House, Southampton, are among the archives of The Queen's College, Oxford (deposited in the Bodleian Library), which took over custody of the house in 1347. The English estates of Bec Abbey, in Normandy, came to the Crown by the act suppressing alien priories in 1414, but most of their manors were given to Eton College and King's College, Cambridge, and the manorial records passed to them and remain in their archives. This shows how an institution's archives may well include manorial records older than its own foundation. At the dissolution a monastery's estates may have passed more or less intact to a new owner, and its manorial records into his archives. Thus the surviving manorial records from Glastonbury Abbey (Somerset) are in the archives of the Marquess of Bath at Longleat (Wiltshire), and those from Crowland Abbey (Lincolnshire) are among the records of Queens' College, Cambridge (deposited in Cambridge University Library). Sometimes the estates had a more complicated history, but the manorial records still remained, if not all together, at least in very substantial blocks; the Public Record

Office and the British Library together hold most of those from Eynsham Abbey (Oxfordshire) and from Ramsey Abbey (Huntingdonshire). More often, however, the monasteries' manorial records have been fragmented with their estates, and surviving groups are apt to relate to only one or two manors; they may be in private possession, or deposited in a local record office, or they may have passed to the British Library or another national repository.

So too with most surviving medieval manorial records from lay estates. There are very few estates indeed that have remained with their records in the hands of a single family from the middle ages to the present. Nearly all the medieval lay estates from which we have anything like intact archives are those that passed into the hands of the Crown; the records that were taken over with the lands are now, if they survive at all, in the Public Record Office. Among them are substantial collections of manorial records from the estates of Isabella de Fortibus, countess of Aumâle, which she made over to King Edward I on her deathbed in 1293, and those of Roger Bigod, earl of Norfolk, which escheated to the Crown in 1306. Quite outstanding are the records of the duchy of Lancaster, which came to the Crown when Henry Bolingbroke became king in 1399. Their importance is enhanced by the sheer size and geographical extent of the estate: in 1399 it was the largest private estate in England and extended into many counties, with particular strength in Lancashire, Derbyshire, Lincolnshire and Yorkshire. It continued to be run separately from the other Crown estates and there survive in the public records series of its manorial records that continue throughout the fifteenth century and later. The duchy of Cornwall and the earldom of Chester, effectively in the hands of the Crown from the thirteenth century, were likewise kept apart from other royal estates and from them too we have some medieval manorial records, but from other estates of the Crown we have far fewer than their size and importance would lead us to expect; mostly they were managed indirectly, through the sheriffs and other officials, and they have left few records of their administration. However, when manors temporarily in the Crown's hands were entrusted to a sheriff or other custodian answerable for all receipts and expenses, a financial account would be presented each year at the Exchequer; this would be included in the annual Pipe Roll or (from 1368) a separate series of Foreign Accounts, that is accounts for business lying outside the sheriffs' regular administration.

Where an estate has continued in single ownership from the middle ages onwards it will have not only medieval manorial records but later manorial court records as well. Post-medieval records of manorial courts are also to be found in the estate papers of a great many other families and institutions. There are often good series for Crown manors because by the mid sixteenth century the auditors of royal land revenue were ordering stewards to bring their court rolls to the audit each year and to lodge them locally for safe keeping in a designated place of deposit.[10] And far more often than earlier manorial records they survive in substantial or even complete series in the possession of private landowners or deposited in local record offices. In 1922 the Law of Property Act abolished the form of land tenure known as copyhold which had been administered through manorial courts. Because manorial records might be needed as evidence of title to former copyhold land the Law of Property (Amendment) Act, 1924, stated that 'All manorial documents shall be under the charge and superintendence of the

---

[10] I owe this information to the kindness of Dr C.J. Kitching.

Master of the Rolls' and gave the Master of the Rolls power to draw up rules for the control and custody of manorial records. This he did in the Manorial Documents Rules, 1926, subsequently replaced by the revised Manorial Documents Rules, 1959, which with minor amendments in 1963 and 1967 are still in force.[11] They require the lord of a manor to keep safely all manorial documents under his control, and to give particulars of them to the Master of the Rolls on request; if any are damaged or decayed, or if they pass to a new owner, the secretary of the Historical Manuscripts Commission is to be told; unless the Master of the Rolls agrees they may not be taken outside England and Wales, the limit of his jurisdiction; they may be deposited in a record repository approved for the purpose by the Master of the Rolls, and in this case the authority controlling the repository is required to send a list of the documents, in set form, both to the lord of the manor and to the secretary of the Historical Manuscripts Commission, as well as to make the documents available for specified purposes including (if the lord of the manor agrees) historical research. Manorial documents are thus one of the very few types of historical record in England and Wales to have some form of legal protection. What we have taken as manorial records is both wider and narrower than manorial documents as defined for this purpose: 'court rolls, surveys, maps, terriers, documents and books of every description relating to the boundaries, wastes, customs or courts of a manor', specifically excluding the title-deeds of the manor and any document of later date than 1925. To implement these rules the Master of the Rolls set up a Register of Manorial Documents recording their ownership and location; this is maintained on his behalf by the Historical Manuscripts Commission.

The Register of Manorial Documents is available for public inspection in the Commission's offices (Quality House, Quality Court, Chancery Lane, London WC2). It is arranged by counties, and within each county alphabetically by manors, along with honours, hundreds and other units of private jurisdiction; a separate index gives cross-references from the names of parishes to the manors each contained. Taken in conjunction with the National Register of Archives, also maintained by the Historical Manuscripts Commission, it is an invaluable guide to surviving manorial records, especially the more widespread records of the post-medieval manorial courts. Within a particular area the published or unpublished catalogues of those private estate archives that have been deposited in the county record office or other repository are an obvious guide to those available locally; for areas covered by its published topographical volumes the *Victoria History of the Counties of England* (the '*V.C.H.*') can be used to discover what manorial records exist and where they are to be found. Most of the manorial records in the Public Record Office have been separated from their archival contexts and formed into three of the artificial groups of records known as Special Collections – Rentals and Surveys (SC11 and SC12), Ministers' Accounts (SC6; by minister is meant any bailiff or other official) and Court Rolls (SC2) and for each there is a published list.[12] These records are kept in the central London

---

[11] Statutory Rules and Orders 1925/1310; Statutory Instruments 1959/1399, 1963/976, 1967/963. These should be read together with section 144A in schedule 2 of the 1924 act: 15 George V, c.5.

[12] *Public Record Office: Lists and Indexes*, 5 and 34 (ministers' accounts, parts I and II, 1894, 1910), 6 and supplementary series 5, vol.i (court rolls, 1896, 1964), 25 and supplementary series 14 (rentals and surveys, 1908, 1968). There are unpublished lists in the P.R.O. itself of subsequent additions to the classes covered in these volumes as well as of the manorial records in other classes (e.g. the court rolls in the Chancery Masters' Exhibits and in the Office of the Auditors of Land Revenue: C116, LR3).

section of the Office: Chancery Lane, London WC2. The convenience of these groupings is far outweighed by our being no longer able to tell how or when a particular manorial record came into the hands of the Crown or what were the original archive groups (only those from the duchy of Lancaster are distinguished from the rest though included in the same published lists). There is also a published list of the Foreign Accounts, covering both those on the Pipe Rolls and those in the separate series.[13] Manorial records in the Department of Manuscripts of the British Library, Reference Division (formerly British Museum), are mostly among the various collections of rolls and charters, of which the Additional Charters and Additional Rolls (which form a single numerical sequence) are by far the largest; these last are listed, and places indexed, in successive volumes of the *Catalogue of Additions*, while there is a separate published place index to all charters and rolls that were in the British Museum in 1900.[14] After the foundation of local record offices from the late 1920s onwards relatively few manorial records were acquired by the British Museum; notable exceptions are those in the Shrewsbury (Talbot) and Thoresby Park archives.[15]

Notes of selected editions of manorial records are given at the end of each chapter. Despite their length and the difficulty of abridging or calendaring them satisfactorily, quite a number of medieval manorial records are now in print, either in the original Latin or in translation, in editions that vary greatly in their thoroughness and reliability. A particular stimulus was given by F.W. Maitland who, in his edition of *Select Pleas in Manorial and Other Seignorial Courts*, Selden Soc. ii (1889), emphasised the interest and historical importance of these texts; but precursors included editions of *The Domesday of St. Paul's of the Year MCCXXII* by W.H. Hale, Camden Soc. [Old Ser.] lxix (1858), of *Two Compoti of the Lancashire and Cheshire Manors of Henry de Lacy, Earl of Lincoln* by P.A. Lyons, Chetham Soc. [Old Ser.] cxii (1884) and of *Custumals of Battle Abbey* by S.R. Scargill-Bird, Camden Soc. New Ser. xli (1887). An interesting experiment in calendaring, which merits careful attention, is A.F.C. Baber's *The Court Rolls of the Manor of Bromsgrove and King's Norton 1494–1504*, Worcestershire Historical Soc. (1963). On the whole editors have tended to select for publication the early records in any series. This has produced some imbalance among the published texts; even for the fifteenth century we are far from having a fully representative range of manorial records in print, while later manorial court records have mostly been neglected by publishing societies. The ambitious project of the Yorkshire Archaeological Society to publish the court rolls of the manor of Wakefield from all periods deserves to be copied elsewhere.

The select texts listed at the end of each subsequent chapter are not intended as full lists of even the best published editions; they are meant simply as specimens of the various types of manorial records, specimens that cannot be published here because of their length. Availability, quality of editing, variety of type of document in both Latin text and translation, chronological and geographical coverage, have all been taken into account in selection.[16] The plates, illustrating

[13] *Public Record Office: Lists and indexes*, 11 (1900).

[14] *Index to the Charters and Rolls in the Department of Manuscripts, British Museum*, ed. H.J. Ellis and F.B Bickley (London, 2v., 1900–12).

[15] Respectively Add. Charters 72121–74194 and Egerton Charters 2301–8836.

[16] Outstanding among those that fail to meet the test of availability is the superb edition of accounts and court rolls from Ramsey Abbey's manor of Elton (Hunts.): *Elton Manorial Records 1279–1351*, ed. S.C. Ratcliff (privately printed for the Roxburghe Club, 1946).

typical manorial records, have been chosen from the manuscripts of these select texts, so that they can be compared with the documents in edited and printed form. Useful guides to further published records are R. Somerville, *Handlist of Record Publications*, British Records Association, Publications Pamphlet, 3 (1951), E.L.C. Mullins, *Texts and Calendars*, Royal Historical Soc., Guides and Handbooks, 7 and 12 (1958, 1983), and E.B. Graves, *A Bibliography of English History to 1485* (Oxford, 1975), pp.666–90.

The tools for the job
One essential tool for the job of using manorial records is, self-evidently, some knowledge of the language in which they are written. This language is Latin – among the medieval records almost without exception. In the fifteenth century we find a very few financial records of estates written in English or French, a few estate surveys in English and some by-laws or local ordinances entered in English on manorial court rolls that are otherwise entirely in Latin. Letters on estate business were often written in French from the late thirteenth century onwards, and in English in the fifteenth century. Treatises of the thirteenth and fourteenth centuries on estate management, auditing accounts and holding manorial courts are mostly written in French, but, significantly, those instructing the clerks who actually wrote the court rolls and accounts are always in Latin. With these few exceptions all surviving records of medieval estate administration, all medieval manorial records, are written in Latin, and so too are most of the formal records of proceedings in later manorial courts until an act of 1731 required them to be written in English.

Knowledge of Latin is thus essential for anyone who works on manorial records before the eighteenth century, but this should not deter those who did not learn the language of Vergil and Cicero in their schooldays. Indeed those who did will still have something to learn before they are familiar with the language of manorial documents, for although it follows fairly closely the basic grammatical rules of classical Latin, its vocabulary is very different, containing many words drawn from English (sometimes in latinised form, sometimes not) and many words that are used with technical meanings peculiar to medieval administrative records in general or to manorial records in particular. To learn the language of these records even without a prior knowledge of classical Latin is not dauntingly difficult, and Eileen A. Gooder, *Latin for Local History* (2nd edn, London, 1978), is an excellent introduction, for complete beginners, to the grammar and vocabulary of English medieval records. Translated records have been included in the lists of select texts because they can be helpful when one is trying to learn the Latin of manorial records, whether as a newcomer to the language or as an experienced classical Latinist.

As relatively few manorial records have been published almost anyone working on them is going to have to read the actual manuscripts, so a knowledge of palaeography is another necessary tool for the job. This too is not nearly so difficult as it may seem at first sight and, like Latin, it is essential to acquire ready competence in it: manorial records offer quite enough difficulties in interpretation without adding to them by faulty reading or faulty Latin. There are several excellent introductions to the handwriting of English medieval records, such as L.C. Hector, *The Handwriting of English Documents* (2nd edn, London, 1966; reissued Dorking, 1980). Some actual instruction can be helpful in learning palaeography; courses are often offered by university extra-mural departments or other organisations, and enquiry at any local record office will produce information about any that are available in the area.

Further reading
The only book that deals with manorial records in general is N.J. Hone, *The Manor and Manorial Records* (London, 1906); though out-of-date in some respects it includes much useful information, along with specimen texts in translation, lists of court rolls in several major repositories and a bibliography that includes a substantial number of local publications. R.H. Hilton, 'The Content and Sources of English Agrarian History before 1500', *Ag.H.R.* iii (1955), pp.3–19, puts manorial records in the context of other available sources. Titow, *Rural Soc.*, discusses the records from 1200–1350 and the problems on which they throw light, with a useful collection of texts, mostly manorial records, in translation.

The suggestions for further reading at the end of subsequent chapters are confined to works dealing in general with the particular type of record, and make no attempt to cover historical studies that are based, even directly and solely, on manorial records. These are very numerous, for among them are nearly all works on the social and economic history of the medieval countryside; often they include important discussion of the particular records that they use, and anyone working on manorial records would be well advised to become acquainted with what has been written on these subjects – and not just with what has been written recently, for there is much wisdom still not fully recognised or exploited in the works of the pioneers in this field: F. Seebohm, F.W. Maitland, P. Vinogradoff and others. More recent work has included studies of particular estates, particular regions and particular places in medieval England, and contrasting examples in each category in turn are: I. Kershaw, *Bolton Priory: the Economy of a Northern Monastery 1286–1325* (London, 1973), and C. Dyer, *Lords and Peasants in a Changing Society: the Estates of the Bishopric of Worcester, 680–1540* (Cambridge, 1980); H.C. Darby, *The Medieval Fenland* (2nd edn, Newton Abbot, 1974), and R.H. Hilton, *A Medieval Society: the West Midlands at the End of the Thirteenth Century* (London, 1966); P.D.A Harvey, *A Medieval Oxfordshire Village: Cuxham, 1240–1400* (London, 1965), and Z. Razi, *Life, Marriage and Death in a Medieval Parish: Economy, Society and Demography in Halesowen 1270–1400* (Cambridge, 1980). There are also monographs on particular aspects of the subject, and recent examples include work on the peasantry, such as R.H. Hilton, *The English Peasantry in the Later Middle Ages* (Oxford, 1975), on agrarian organisation, such as *Studies of Field Systems in the British Isles*, ed. A.R.H. Baker and R.A. Butlin (Cambridge, 1973), and on corn production: J.Z. Titow, *Winchester Yields* (Cambridge, 1972). E.B Graves, *A Bibliography of English History to 1485* (Oxford, 1975), is an invaluable guide to work published before 1971.

CHAPTER II

SURVEYS

Introduction

A medieval survey is a written description of property. Drawing a map or plan was no part of the surveyor's business (indeed, maps and plans were practically unknown in medieval England) and only two pre-sixteenth-century surveys are known that have any sort of plan associated with them: from Shouldham (Norfolk) in 1440–1 and from Tanworth-in-Arden (Warwickshire) about 1500. In both cases the plans were among the surveyor's notes and drafts, not part of his final survey.[1] Most surveys were meant to last: they would be used for reference by estate administrators for a whole generation or more, and consequently we find that, far more than other manorial records, they are apt to be copied into cartularies or registers where they would be permanently and conveniently at hand – early examples include the twelfth-century surveys in the principal surviving cartulary of Ramsey Abbey (Huntingdonshire) and the register containing early-thirteenth-century surveys of the bishop of Lincoln's estates.[2] Not only were surveys kept and copied; they might also be brought up to date, perfectly or imperfectly, either by annotation or else by wholesale revision, putting present tenants' names for the former ones and making other necessary alterations. Thus an early-thirteenth-century survey of Combe (Berkshire) survives in five successive versions; on the earliest are some added notes and other alterations, and the others incorporate in the text of the survey these and other later changes.[3] In the fourteenth and fifteenth centuries it was usual on many estates to compile surveys at frequent, even regular, intervals – so much so that it became common practice for any survey to be described in its heading as renewed (*renovatum*), often meaning no more than, simply, compiled.

Where we are told who drew up a survey it seems normally to have been the work not of a single surveyor but of a committee: a group of local tenants and others who gave the information on oath and who are sometimes named on the survey itself, more often referred to obliquely – 'as the jurors say'. In post-medieval manorial records the work of surveying is often closely associated with the manorial court; it is not clear whether medieval surveys were normally drawn up in the court, though sometimes the acknowledgments of tenants' customs systematically entered on the court roll amount to a form of survey.[4] Nor is it clear what procedure was followed when a survey involved actual measurement, though very occasionally we hear of officials brought to a manor to measure land; these would be men more experienced than the local jurors in the techniques of mensuration, but we find no trace of professional surveyors in England before the sixteenth century.[5]

There are several types of medieval survey and we shall look at each in turn. At first sight they all seem very straightforward documents, with fewer obvious technicalities than either manorial accounts or court rolls. In fact it is often

[1] *Local Maps*, pp.17–18, 195–201, 317–28.
[2] *Cart. Mon. Ram.* iii, pp.237–314 passim; The Queen's College, Oxford, MS.366.
[3] *Bec Docs.* pp.41–5.
[4] e.g. *Cuxham Man. Recs.* pp.656–9 (a court roll of 1329).
[5] *Local Maps*, pp.14, 16.

15

difficult to be sure that one has interpreted a survey correctly, largely because of
the ambiguities in the terms used for the units by which land is described or
measured. Difficulties stem above all from the word acre (Latin *acra*). In some
areas local usage poses particular problems; in Cornwall, for instance, there was
the so-called Cornish acre which usually contained from 40 to 60 statute acres.[6]
Generally, however, we have to reckon with three possible meanings of the word:

(1) The customary acre, referred to in the records as field acre or acre as it lies
(*acra campestris*, *acra ut iacet*). A strip of land in an arable field, based on the
selion (*selio*), the strip often more or less ridged that was formed by the action
of ploughing, but of no particular area; what was called an acre in any
particular field or part of a field might consist of one, two or more of these
selions. Sometimes, confusingly, a small strip would be called a half-acre, a
very small one a quarter-acre or rood, but this does not imply a specific area of
measurement of any kind.

(2) The measured acre (*acra mensurata*). An area of land which was often
defined (remembering the acre's strip-shaped origin) as 40 perches long by 4
perches wide but which could of course be any shape containing 160 square
perches; references occur in the twelfth and early thirteenth centuries to
3-perch and 5-perch measured acres, that is to acres of 120 and 200 square
perches respectively, but these seem to have been local and temporary
aberrations. Where the perch measured 16½ feet this was thus the modern
statute acre, but local perches of various lengths might be used (perches of
from 15 to 20 feet were quite normal) and woodland in particular was often
measured with a longer perch than arable, even in a single survey.

(3) The fiscal acre. Not, strictly speaking, a piece of land at all, but a unit of
tax assessment; both the hide and the carucate, the two most usual units used
to define liability to tax in eleventh-century England, could be divided into
(normally) 120 of these so-called acres, but as neither hide nor carucate
comprised a fixed area of land neither too did the fiscal acre. A holding
described as 10 such acres might be presumed to be larger than a 5-acre
holding in the same place, but all we can say for certain is that it paid twice as
much tax. By the end of the twelfth century this assessment system was no
longer used for taxation but the fiscal acres remained as traditional descriptions
of holdings, descriptions which tell us nothing of either a holding's measured
area or the number of its arable strips. These descriptions might involve
minute, even fractional, acreages where a holding had been divided.

Very occasionally a survey will say if its acres are customary or measured ones
but usually it gives no explicit indication of the kind of acres it is using in
describing property. But, though all three sorts of acre might be divided into
half-acres and quarter-acres (or roods), if a survey divides acres even further into
(square) perches we can be sure that we are dealing with measured acres.[7] And
any trace of uniform acreage between holdings taken either singly or in groups of
two or three will normally mean that fiscal acres are being used, though
occasionally a reallocation of a vill's lands could produce holdings that were
identical even in their measured area. Despite these guidelines it is often difficult

---

[6] J. Hatcher, *Rural Economy and Society in the Duchy of Cornwall 1300–1500* (Cambridge,
1970), p.18n.

[7] Other subdivisions of the measured acre are found in some areas, such as the daywork of 4
square perches (Essex, Kent and elsewhere) and the pall of 20 square perches (Sussex).

to tell what sort of acre a survey is using. It is only if we know that the acres are measured acres and if we know the length of perch that was used that we can interpret the acres of a medieval survey as definable units of area – a fact that far too many historians.have found it convenient to ignore.

They can, however, call in their defence certain medieval writers whose own ideas on the subject were far from clear, particularly in relation to two other terms often used in surveys, bovate and virgate. Both belong to the same system of tax assessment as the fiscal acre. The bovate (or oxgang) was one-eighth of the carucate, the primary unit throughout much of eastern and northern England; the virgate (or yardland) was one-quarter of the hide, the primary unit of assessment over most of the rest of the country. Like the fiscal acre, both words continued in use long after their role in tax assessment had ceased (indeed oxgangs and yardlands both survived to the nineteenth century) and each meant simply a standard peasant holding in a particular community.[8] Very often all the bovates or virgates in a village owed the lord of the manor exactly the same rents and services but it did not follow that they all comprised precisely the same amount of land. Sometimes groups of small or very small holdings were called half-virgates (or semi-virgates) or quarter-virgates (or quarterlands) but this again did not imply any sort of measurement. The half-virgate in one village need not be smaller than the full virgate in another: they were descriptive terms, not units of measurement. Normally the virgate comprised 30 fiscal acres, the bovate 15. But some texts try to force measured or customary acres into a single system with virgates and hides, bovates and carucates; thus one fifteenth-century treatise on accounting tells us that '4 virgates of land make a hide and 25 acres make a virgate and 40 perches in length and 4 in breadth make an acre'.[9]

However, in the thirteenth century, when measurement of land started to become a normal practice on many estates, some administrators left notes of the actual area of land in a virgate, recognising that this would vary from one manor to another, and even between holdings on a single manor. Thus thirteenth-century surveys in the Ramsey Abbey cartulary say for each manor how many acres there are in the virgate, even if only approximately; at Cranfield (Bedford-shire), for instance, some virgates contained 48 acres, some were smaller. The same cartulary contains a separate list of the size in acres of each manor's virgates; these do not entirely correspond to the acreage as given in each survey, reflecting the variation between one virgate and another and the impossibility of giving a precise figure for all the virgates even on one manor.[10]

This may seem to have been a needlessly technical and inconclusive discussion, but it must be remembered that acres and either virgates or bovates are key words in nearly all medieval surveys and that a proper understanding of the entire survey will depend on interpreting these words correctly. Often we cannot be sure we have got the answer right, but at least we can be aware of the traps that lie in wait for us.

Custumals and demesne surveys
The very few estate surveys, mostly fragments, that survive from before the

---

[8] In Kent the assessment unit was the sulung of 4 yokes; the yoke (*iugum*) was used as the name for a standard holding but early fragmentation meant that by the late thirteenth century it had little more than a notional existence.

[9] *Henley*, p.475.

[10] *Cart. Mon. Ram.* i, p.438; iii, pp.208–15 (cf., for Upwood, i, p.343).

Norman Conquest follow a single pattern: apart from the hidage, the property's assessment for taxation, the information they give us is entirely about the local peasant tenants and the rents and services that they owed their landlord.[11] They are custumals, a form of survey which was still being drawn up in the fourteenth century and which consists of a list of a manor's tenants with the customs – the customary obligations – under which each held his house and lands (see Plate 1). On some manors entire classes of tenants owed more or less uniform customs, and here the custumal will set them out in full for one of their number as a paradigm, the other tenants being said to hold on the same terms or with only minor variations; on other manors there was no such uniformity and each tenant's obligations had to be listed individually. Good examples of each sort are among the custumals drawn up about 1230 for the English manors of Bec Abbey (Normandy): at Combe (Berkshire) William White and Osbert Oppere are taken as specimen virgater and half-virgater respectively, their fellow-tenants simply being listed as holding in the same way, while at Blakenham (Suffolk) there was such variation between one tenant and another that they nearly all had to have their services set out separately.[12]

Domesday Book, the royal survey of 1086 covering nearly the whole country, tells us nothing of tenants' obligations. It records how many tenants there were on each manor and, in terms of their total number of ploughteams, the amount of land they held altogether, and for the manor as a whole it gives the tax assessment in hides or carucates and their subdivisions, as well as the manor's annual value in 1066 and at the time of the survey. For the rest, however, it is concerned only with the manorial demesne, its area of arable in terms of ploughteams, its meadows and woodlands, its mills, fisheries and (though omitted from the final version) its livestock. Domesday Book lies outside our scope – a handbook the same length as this could give only the simplest introduction to its complexities – but it is important in the history of private estate surveys in England for two reasons. First, a few estate holders based surveys of their own on the information gathered for Domesday Book; some, like Ely Abbey and St Augustine's Priory, Canterbury, had copies made of the Domesday returns as first collected by the royal commissioners, while others, like Canterbury Cathedral Priory, simply drew on this information for more original compilations of their own.[13] Second, the Domesday survey at least spread, and may have introduced, the idea of including in manorial surveys information about demesne lands, particularly the number of teams needed to plough the arable and lists of livestock; we find this in the surveys of 1114–18 from Burton Abbey (Staffordshire),[14] and by the end of the twelfth century some description of the demesne lands had become a normal prelude to the custumal in any manorial survey. Thus, surveys made for St Paul's Cathedral in 1222 give for each manor the acreage (probably in customary acres) of demesne arable, meadow, pasture and woods.[15]

[11] Agnes J. Robertson, *Anglo-Saxon Charters* (2nd edn, Cambridge, 1956), pp.164–9, 204–7.
[12] *Bec Docs.* pp.40–5, 92–6.
[13] *Libri Censualis vocati Domesday-Book Additamenta* (Record Commission, 1816), pp.497–528; *An Eleventh-Century Inquisition of St. Augustine's, Canterbury*, ed. A. Ballard, British Academy, Records of Social and Economic History, 4 (1920); *The Domesday Monachorum of Christ Church Canterbury*, ed. D.C. Douglas (London, 1944).
[14] 'The Burton Abbey Twelfth Century Surveys', ed. C.G.O. Bridgeman, *Collections for a History of Staffordshire 1916*, William Salt Archaeological Soc. (1918), pp.212–47 (Survey B).
[15] *Dom. St. Paul's.*

Comprehensive twelfth-century surveys survive from only about a dozen estates, all of them belonging to large ecclesiastical landlords – from Peterborough Abbey about 1125, from the bishopric of Durham in 1183 (the Boldon Book), from the Templars' estates in England in 1185, and so on.[16] All are of great historical importance, especially where, from Burton Abbey and Ramsey Abbey, we have surveys of the same estate at two different dates. There are also a very few twelfth-century surveys of other individual manors, such as the royal manors of Aylesbury and Brill (Buckinghamshire).[17] From 1200, the number of surveys surviving (and almost certainly the number actually produced) rapidly increases, and by the late thirteenth century the manorial survey was already a normal part of estate administration, a change probably connected with the spread of demesne farming: efficient management demanded that the landlord should know precisely what his local resources were. This need for precision led to a further development: the use of actual measurement in describing the manorial demesne lands. This probably began in the 1230s, when measured acres first appear in manorial accounts. We can see this change in comparing two successive thirteenth-century treatises on estate management: the *Rules* of Robert Grosseteste, of 1240–2, simply recommend the landlord to have surveys made of his tenants' lands and of his manorial demesnes, but the *Seneschaucy*, which probably dates from the middle of the century or a little later, says that the estate steward 'ought to arrange for all the demesne lands, of each manor, to be measured by lawful men. He ought to know by the perch of the country how many acres there are in each field.'[18]

We must be wary of believing everything a custumal tells us about tenants' rents and services. Its aim is to set out the theoretical obligations of the tenant: what he actually rendered was not necessarily the same. The custumal may show that he owed labour services for his land: so many days' work each week throughout the year, perhaps with particular services of ploughing, hay-making or reaping at busy seasons. But manorial accounts for the same places may well show that the lord regularly 'sold' these works to the tenant – that is, he made a money payment instead. Custumals are a very unsafe guide to the prevalence of labour services. Even where services were actually rendered we must not be misled by the custumal's phraseology: 'he shall work two days every week' normally means that the tenant has to provide someone to do the work, not that he need do it in person. This may well emerge from the same document if the tenant's personal presence is explicitly required on particular occasions: 'He shall work with two men at harvest and shall watch over them to see that they work well'. Again, where a custumal calls for rents in produce at particular seasons they may really have been paid in cash instead; if we are told that a manor's tenants owed an annual render of oats we cannot even say for certain that oats were grown there at all at that period. Generally speaking, manorial accounts, if they survive, provide a useful check on much of what a custumal tells us, though, as we shall see, accounts pose problems of their own. But apart from these difficulties over the more practical obligations set out in custumals we must

---

[16] A useful list is given by M.M. Postan, 'The Chronology of Labour Services', *T.R.H.S.* 4th Ser. xx (1937), p.175n.

[17] G.H. Fowler, 'Extents of the Royal Manors of Aylesbury and Brill, circa 1155', *Records of Bucks.* xi (1920–6), pp.401–5. They are not, strictly speaking, extents.

[18] *Henley*, pp.388–9, 264–5.

remember that some of their obligations may have been very theoretical indeed. The virgater of Combe had to collect provisions from the market if they should be needed when the abbot of Bec visited his manor, but the contingency was, to say the least, an unlikely one.[19] The bond tenants of the bishop of Durham at West Auckland in the 1380s were required to erect a lodge, of specified size, for the bishop's hunt; but as we find exactly the same obligation in the Boldon Book two hundred years earlier it was perhaps a piece of traditional verbiage rather than an aspect of the estate's contemporary economy.[20]

Extents

Where the *Seneschaucy* tells the steward to measure the demesne lands, Walter of Henley's *Husbandry*, written rather later in the thirteenth century as a commentary on the earlier text, enjoins the landlord to 'Make an extent of your lands and your tenements by your lawful sworn men'.[21] The change marks the spread of the type of manorial survey known as the extent. The essence of the extent was that every item in it – every building and piece of land on the demesne, every labour service, every rent in produce – had a valuation attached to it, this valuation being the amount that could be got for it annually if it were leased out. Almost certainly the extent originated in the surveys made by royal officials of properties that came into the hands of the Crown. The Crown leased out practically all its estates, so the valuations would show how much the property would be worth if it were retained. The earliest surviving extent in the public records is of 1236, the first of the large and important series of extents made for the Crown; an extent was normally drawn up from the local enquiries (the Inquisition Post Mortem) that followed the death of anyone holding land of the Crown directly.[22] The earliest private extents probably date from the 1240s, and from the middle of the century this type of survey spread rapidly. Two surveys from Stoke sub Hamdon (Somerset), a manor of the Beauchamp family, provide an interesting comparison between an old-style custumal in 1251 and a new-style extent in 1287.[23]

Some extents are no more than simple demesne surveys or custumals with valuations added. But most followed a fixed form that was enshrined in formularies and specimen texts, even in a set of instructions for drawing up an extent which circulated widely and which later lawyers saw as having near-statutory authority; Walter of Henley followed his injunction to make an extent with a synopsis of this text. The formal scheme of an extent is set out in Figure 1 (see also Plate 2). It begins with a description of the manor-house and its surrounding farm buildings, yards and gardens. There follows an account of the demesne arable, measured and valued piece by piece; where a two- or three-field system operated the land in each furlong would be described separately, and a total area and valuation given for each field. Often the extent reads as if it were describing all the arable in a given furlong whereas really it is referring only to the demesne land; at this point in the extent the tenants are entirely ignored. After the arable the demesne meadow, pasture, woodland and other appurtenances are described in turn (some minor variations occur in the exact order of these items).

---

[19] *Bec Docs.* p.41.
[20] *Hatfield Surv.* p.30; *V.C.H. Durham*, i, p.333.
[21] *Henley*, pp.312–13.
[22] They are noted in the published *Calendar of Inquisitions Post Mortem* (16v., 1904–74), which goes down to 1392.
[23] *Beauchamp Regs.* pp.2–24.

MANOR HOUSE and its gardens, grounds and dovecotes: annual value of each item
    'TOTAL value

MILLS: annual value of each
    TOTAL value

DEMESNE ARABLE
    First field: area of demesne and annual value for each furlong in turn
      Sub-total
    Second field: area of demesne and annual value for each furlong in turn
      Sub-total
      TOTAL area and value

DEMESNE MEADOW: area and annual value of demesne strips
    TOTAL area and value

DEMESNE PASTURE AND WOODS: area and annual value of each piece
    TOTAL area and value

TENANTS' RENTS AND SERVICES: obligations (labour, produce, cash) of each tenant in
turn, giving annual value
    TOTAL value

    TOTAL VALUE OF MANOR

Figure 1. Scheme of a manorial extent

The extent then concludes with a custumal of the tenants and their services, a custumal that includes a valuation of every item. The tenants' lands are not measured and described as the demesne lands are: the extent is concerned with the property solely from the viewpoint of the manorial lord and his profit, and whereas on the demesne this profit came from exploiting the land directly the profit from the tenants' holdings came from the tenants themselves, and the extent needed to look no further.

In its meticulous description and measurement of the manorial demesne the extent typifies the period of demesne farming and the care that the efficient landlord would take to watch over his local resources so as to draw maximum profits from them. It is an odd irony that the extent's valuations should relate to leasing, the alternative system of estate management, and this means that these valuations in a private extent may be more or less artificial. It is reasonable to take, say, differences in the value of an arable acre from one furlong to another in the same extent as reflecting real differences in the quality of the land; it is much riskier to make similar comparisons between extents from different manors or to assume that if parcels of demesne land were leased out (as increasingly happened in the fourteenth century) the rents charged would correspond to the valuations of the extent. But not all these valuations need be artificial; the manorial accounts show that the tenants' harvest works at Farleigh (Surrey) were remitted for amounts very close to the valuation entered on extents of the manor.[24]

It may be that landlords found the valuations of an extent unhelpful and meaningless when they came to lease out their demesne lands and other assets in a fluctuating market; or it may be simply that the decline in demesne farming reduced the need for such comprehensive surveys. At any rate the number of

---

[24] Muniments of Merton College, Oxford, 4797–4849, 4889–4895, passim. I owe this information and these references to the kindness of Mr T.H. Aston and Mr R. Evans.

private extents falls off rapidly after the middle of the fourteenth century. This is
not to say that the extent disappeared. One surviving model extent dates from the
reign of Henry VI.[25] But the surveys most characteristic of the fourteenth and
fifteenth centuries were not extents but terriers and rentals.

Terriers

A terrier is a description of lands that follows a topographical arrangement,
proceeding parcel by parcel through the fields, crofts and meadows. The part of
an extent that describes the demesne lands is in effect a terrier with valuations,
and a simple demesne terrier follows just this form. An example is one from
Cuxham (Oxfordshire) in 1447–8: the demesne lands in each furlong of the three
open fields are listed in turn, in this case giving both the number of customary
acres and their measurements on the ground, and, as we have seen in extents, it
reads, misleadingly, as if it were describing the whole of each furlong whereas in
fact its acreages and measurements relate only to the demesne strips.[26] A terrier of
this sort need not, of course, be of manorial demesne lands: often we find terriers
of the lands of an individual tenant, whether held of a single manor or of two or
more manorial lords. Often, indeed, what amounts to a terrier of a free tenant's
lands is incorporated in a written conveyance. A grant made about 1270 of two
40-acre holdings in Cambridge and Chesterton (Cambridgeshire) lists in great
detail and at great length the individual pieces of land they comprised; another of
1443 describes in full the 74 ploughing-strips (selions: *seliones*) that made up a
free estate in Corby and Swinstead (both Lincolnshire).[27]

Some terriers of the late fourteenth or fifteenth century cover all the lands of a
vill, or other group of fields, even though they belong to more than one manorial
lord. An early and notable example is the terrier of the West Fields of Cambridge
that dates from about 1370; it describes, strip by strip, over a thousand separate
parcels of land in an arable area of uncertain (possibly divided) manorial lordship,
in the hands of many different occupiers and divided between several different
parishes.[28] A later, rather simpler, terrier of this sort comes from Thame
(Oxfordshire) about 1450, describing the lands of two manorial lords, Thame
Abbey and Drew Barantyne.[29] These composite terriers are not uncommon; they
have never been studied as a group and would well repay investigation. Knowing
why and how they were drawn up might well add significantly to our knowledge
of the late-medieval rural community and its internal organisation.

Rentals

A rental is a list of tenants with the amounts of rent (in cash or produce) due from
each. On a manor that consisted entirely of rent-paying town houses there is little
more that any survey could say, and some of the earliest rentals are in fact for
urban properties. The survey of royal property in Winchester about 1110 is a
rental,[30] and a tradition of urban surveys of this sort continued throughout the

[25] P.R.O. E 163/24/34.
[26] *Cuxham Man. Recs.* pp.112–15.
[27] Muniments of Merton College, Oxford, 1606; B.L. Add. Charter 62603.
[28] *Cambridge Fields.*
[29] *The Thame Cartulary*, ed. H.E Salter, Oxfordshire Record Soc. xxv, xxvi, (1947–8), ii,
pp.174–92.
[30] 'The Winton Domesday', ed. F. Barlow, in *Winchester in the Early Middle Ages*, ed. M.
Biddle (Oxford, 1976), pp.32–68.

middle ages. An interesting fifteenth-century example comes from Gloucester in 1455: the properties are listed in topographical order, with thumbnail sketches of churches and other landmarks at the appropriate places.[31]

Often it was convenient for the rural landowner too to compile straightforward lists of tenants and the rents they owed. Medieval rents in cash were commonly due four times a year, not necessarily in equal instalments, while any one rent in produce was normally paid on a single annual occasion. This made it easy to set out a rental as a table. In 1329 Henry de Bray, who held various free properties let out to tenants at Harlestone (Northamptonshire), entered in his memorandum book a list of his tenants, with their rents at Easter, Midsummer, Michaelmas and Christmas in four columns on the opposite page.[32] Many other rentals take a similar form (see Plate 3). One of the lordship of Oswestry (Shropshire) in 1393 sets out in three columns the customary dues of *tunke*, *morkie* and *cantidion* owed by the Welsh rural tenants.[33]

Whether or not it is set out as a table, the rental at first sight seems quite distinct from the other sorts of survey. When a register from Eynsham Abbey follows a copy of a detailed formal extent of Woodeaton (Oxfordshire) with a rental for the same property at the same date, 1366, the difference is clear: in the rental there is no more than a single-line entry for each tenant, giving his name, his holding (virgate, half-virgate or cottage) and the annual rent, merely referring briefly to the 'certain services' also due from each, whereas in the extent these are set out in full detail.[34] But where, as so often by the fifteenth century, labour services and customary renders of produce had all or mostly been commuted to money rents there would be little to say of a tenant's obligations beyond the amount of money he owed each year. The survey from Fountains Abbey (Yorkshire) in 1495–6 is called a rental by both its compiler and its editor, and much of it is barely more than a list of names and rents; however, some lessees of manors and other substantial properties had more complicated obligations, owing butter, cheese and calves in return for the custody of the abbey's dairy herds, and these are set out in detail with their value.[35] An extent could do no more, and we see how the extent or custumal might be indistinguishable from the rental simply by virtue of the changes in estate management and local tenures that occurred in the late middle ages. The lordship of Oswestry rental of 1393 is in fact entitled an extent. It is a useful reminder that the distinctions we have drawn between the different sorts of medieval survey are not always entirely clear-cut in practice.

The rental might also be indistinguishable from a financial account. The list of rents was, after all, a list of the annual receipts due from the manor or other property; it needed no more than a note at the end of any that could not be collected and of the costs of collection to turn it into the rent collector's account for the year, and on some estates we find rentals, entitled thus, being drawn up every year to serve as accounts rather than as surveys.[36]

---

[31] *Rental of All the Houses in Gloucester, A.D. 1455*, ed. W.H. Stevenson (Gloucester, 1890).

[32] *The Estate Book of Henry de Bray*, ed. Dorothy Willis, Camden Soc. 3rd Ser. xxvii (1916), pp.52–3.

[33] *The Lordship of Oswestry*, ed. W.J. Slack (Shrewsbury, 1951), pp.153–71.

[34] *Eynsham Cartulary*, ed. H.E. Salter, Oxford Historical Soc. [Old Ser.] xlix, li (1907–8), ii, pp.19–24.

[35] *The Fountains Abbey Rental 1495/6*, ed. D.J.H. Michelmore (privately printed, 1974).

[36] e.g. D. & C. Durham, Almoners' Rentals, Bursars' Rentals, etc.

Select texts

'The Burton Abbey Twelfth Century Surveys', ed. C.G.O. Bridgeman, *Collections for a History of Staffordshire 1916*, William Salt Archaeological Soc. (1918), pp.212–47. Custumals 1114–18 and c.1126. Latin text.

V.C.H. Durham, i, pp.327–41. Boldon Book, custumal of the bishopric of Durham estates, 1183. English translation.

Bec Docs. pp.29–123. Custumals, c.1230–1248. Latin text.

Beauchamp Regs. pp.2–56. Custumal for Stoke sub Hamdon, 1251, and extents for Stoke sub Hamdon and three other manors, 1287. English translation.

Stratton Accts. pp.1–30. Extents of Sevenhampton and Stratton (Wilts.), Upton and Blewberry (Berks.), 1271–7. Latin text.

Cambridge Fields. Terrier, c.1370. Latin text.

Hatfield Surv. Rental of the bishopric of Durham estates, c.1382. Latin text.

A Survey of the Manor of Wye, ed. Helen E. Muhlfeld (New York, 1933). Rental of Wye (Kent), 1452–4. Latin text.

Bolton Rentals, pp.1–18. Rental, 1473. English translation.

Further reading

Other accounts of medieval surveys that cover much the same ground as the present chapter, though with differing emphases and further detail, are in the introductions to *Cuxham Man. Recs.* pp.72–8, and to *Local Maps*, pp.11–19. Valuable works on two basically important elements of many or most surveys are N.Neilson, 'Customary Rents', in *Oxf. Studies*, ii (1910), which is useful as a work of reference on particular local rents, and A.Jones, 'Land Measurement in England, 1150–1350', *Ag.H.R.* xxvii (1979), pp.10–18. R.V. Lennard, 'Early Manorial Juries', *E.H.R.* lxxvii (1962), pp.511–18, discusses the local juries named as compiling some late-twelfth- and early-thirteenth-century surveys. The only type of survey that has been the subject of special study is the extent: R.V. Lennard, 'What is a Manorial Extent?', *E.H.R.* xliv (1929), pp.256–63, and T. Lomas, 'The Manorial Extent', *Journal of the Society of Archivists*, vi (1978–81), pp.260–73. Instructions for making an extent are printed in *Statutes of the Realm* (Record Commission, 11v., 1810–28), i, pp.242–3 (the 'Extenta manerii') and in *Legal and Manorial Formularies . . . in Memory of J.P. Gilson* (privately printed, 1933), pp.25–9, and are discussed by Dorothea Oschinsky in *Henley*, pp.68–72, 155–9; the earliest general treatises on surveying are [J. Fitzherbert], *The Boke of Surveyeng and Improvementes* (London, 1523), and R. Benese, *The Maner of Measurynge of All Maner of Lande* (Southwark, [1537?]).

CHAPTER III

ACCOUNTS

Introduction

The manorial account is a product of demesne farming and it is no coincidence that it appears during the first decade of the thirteenth century, just when this method of estate management was being generally adopted. If the landlord entrusted his manor to a local official who was answerable to him for all moneys received or spent, all the corn and livestock, there would clearly have to be a regular reckoning to show what resources remained in hand and how much cash was due from the official to the lord or vice versa. It is this regular reckoning that the manorial account records: its aim was to show the state of account between the lord and his official, to show how much was owing to one or the other once every transaction had been allowed for.

But although demesne farming depended on a regular reckoning of this sort, this did not have to take the form of a written account. There is every indication that until the mid thirteenth century it was unusual to set down in writing the details of accounts; they would be presented by the local official and examined – audited, that is, heard – by the lord or his representative entirely by word of mouth, with no other aids than counters for the calculations, tally-sticks as vouchers and perhaps a few brief notes as memoranda. The estates from which we do have manorial accounts in the first half of the thirteenth century were mostly very large ones indeed: the two earliest are Canterbury Cathedral Priory (1207–8) and the bishopric of Winchester (1208–9), and others include the bishopric of Worcester, Ramsey Abbey and the honour of Gloucester.[1] It may not be coincidence that several were centred on the Winchester area, among them smaller estates such as Southwick Priory (Hampshire).[2] We have hardly any surviving accounts of this period from small estates elsewhere, though Little Dunmow Priory (Essex) provides an example.[3] Probably not even all large estates produced written manorial accounts before the mid thirteenth century: they seem to have been just beginning at Westminster Abbey in the 1250s and at Durham Cathedral Priory in the 1270s.[4] But from the 1250s onwards the idea seems to have spread very fast, especially in the 1270s and 1280s. The second statute of Westminster in 1285, in setting up a form of action against defaulting bailiffs, assumes that there will be written accounts and by the end of the century they were a normal technique of estate management everywhere, on every type of estate; we find them being produced even for the lord who held only a single manor. Moreover their use continued: they may have taken their origin in demesne farming, but they outlasted it, and we still find manorial accounts in the sixteenth century even though all an estate's manors had long been leased. In

---

[1] *Interdict Documents*, ed. Patricia M. Barnes and W.R. Powell, Pipe Roll Soc. New Ser. xxxiv (1960), pp. 69–80 (roll of manorial receipts from Canterbury Cathedral Priory); *The Pipe Roll of the Bishopric of Winchester, 1208–9*, ed. H. Hall (London, 1903); Bodl. Worcestershire Rolls 4; P.R.O. SC6/875/6 (Broughton, Hunts.: manor of Ramsey Abbey), SC6/1109/6–11 (honour of Gloucester).
[2] Muniments of Winchester College, 14484.
[3] Essex Record Office, D/DM Q2.
[4] To judge, that is, from the forms of the earliest accounts still surviving in each archive.

looking at manorial accounting in detail it is convenient to look separately at each of three phases of development: each has its own techniques and its own particular problems for the historian. But these three phases correspond only very broadly to chronological periods – there is a good deal of overlap between them, for one estate might continue old-fashioned practices long after new forms had come in elsewhere.

By and large a manorial account will exist only in a single copy and will take the form of a roll. Sometimes, as we shall see, both a draft and a final version of an account survive, and sometimes what we have are enrolled accounts: the accounts for all of an estate's manors in a particular year are copied on to a single big roll. Historians sometimes call these enrolled accounts pipe rolls, but they were not so called by contemporaries, and the phrase is misleading for they differ in many respects from the real Pipe Rolls, the annual accounts of the sheriffs and others at the royal Exchequer. It is unusual to find manorial accounts copied into books though it did occasionally happen, as at Bolton Abbey (Yorkshire) where a single volume contained all the manorial accounts from 1286 to 1325,[5] or at Canterbury Cathedral Priory, where the accounts of local officials and farmers were entered in a series of registers from the mid fifteenth century onwards.[6] In enrolled or other copied accounts mistakes in copying sometimes produce mistakes in the arithmetic, but in the accounts that were actually used for the audit mistakes seldom occur: too much depended on the accuracy of the figures and too many people were concerned to check them for errors to go unnoticed.

Very occasionally a collection of manorial accounts will include an imaginary account, a specimen that a clerk would use as a guide; this may not be recognised at first sight, for though it may have been copied from one of the standard specimen accounts that were in circulation it could well have had names of places and people altered to fit the particular estate.[7] These specimens were only one of various contemporary aids to manorial accounting which tell us a good deal about the aims and methods of those concerned. We have some rules or treatises for auditors, telling them what to look for on the account, what points to check, what malpractices to guard against. But most of these aids were meant for the clerks who wrote the accounts and who came to be almost the professional advisers of the officials, intermediaries between them and the auditors. Besides treatises on writing accounts and simple models for the clerk to follow there were more elaborate specimen accounts with interspersed rules and comments. The most remarkable surviving formulary comes from Beaulieu Abbey (Hampshire): the accounts of a single year, 1269–70, for all the abbey's officials who handled money, were copied into a large volume with rules and comments interspersed (those from one group of the abbey's manors were also copied into a second book for local use).[8] This seems to have been meant as a once-for-all written version of accounts that would normally be presented orally, serving as a standard and guide for the auditors.

The Beaulieu Abbey formulary was for a particular estate only, but most

[5] Chatsworth House (Derbs.), MS. 73A (described by I. Kershaw, *Bolton Priory: the Economy of a Northern Monastery 1286–1325* (London, 1973), pp.2–3).

[6] D. & C. Canterbury, Miscellaneous Accounts 4, 6–19.

[7] e.g. B.L. Add. MS. 45896, probably adapted on copying for the estates of the Harcourt family.

[8] B.L. Add. MS. 48978, published as *The Account-book of Beaulieu Abbey*, ed. S.F. Hockey, Camden Soc. 4th Ser. xvi (1975); Bodl. MS. Barlow 49.

CASH Charge
          TOTAL
       Discharge
          TOTAL
          BALANCE

CORN For each type of corn in turn:
       Charge
          TOTAL
       Discharge
          TOTAL
          BALANCE

STOCK For each type of live or dead stock in turn:
       Charge
          TOTAL
       Discharge
          TOTAL
          BALANCE

POSSIBLE FURTHER SECTIONS
       LABOUR SERVICES due and performed
       LAND available and how used
       IMPLEMENTS remaining at end of year

Figure 2. Scheme of a manorial account.

guides to manorial accounting were meant for general use. This helps to explain the extraordinary uniformity of these accounts. In looking at successive phases of manorial accounting we shall be noticing idiosyncrasies and variations of one sort or another, but these occur within the context of a standard pattern that was everywhere the same, from the thirteenth century to the sixteenth. How it originated is not entirely clear – it is already well developed in our earliest examples from Canterbury Cathedral Priory and the bishopric of Winchester – but there are some signs that it may have grown out of the inventories drawn up when the lease of a manor came to an end. The manorial account nearly always covers a single year, usually from Michaelmas (29 September) to Michaelmas; and it is always a charge-discharge account. It lists first the charge, the money the official has to answer for – any sum he still owed from the previous year, what he received (or ought to have received) from rents, from sale of produce, from payments imposed on the manorial court, and so on – and gives the total. It then lists all the occasions of the official's paying out money: purchases of corn or livestock, hire of labour, building repairs and the other expenses of running the demesne, and also any cash handed over to the lord or his representative. This is the discharge, showing what the official has done with the money listed in the charge, and it too is totalled. The balance, the difference between the two totals, is then entered, this being the amount that the official owes the lord or (if the outgoings have exceeded the income) vice versa.

    The formal scheme of a manorial account is set out in Figure 2. Nearly all cover corn as well as cash; most deal with livestock too, and many account for other things as well. For each type of corn or livestock, for every other item on the account, there was an individual charge-discharge account on the same principle as for cash. The amounts of wheat (or barley or other corn) harvested, bought or otherwise acquired would be listed and totalled, then the amounts sown as seed, sold, delivered to the lord or otherwise accounted for; the difference between the two totals would be the amount remaining in the granary. Similarly with livestock; but here matters were a little more complicated. Animals grew up: if we have separate paragraphs for pigs and for piglets, last year's piglets have somehow to become this year's pigs. Sometimes they were simply slipped into the pigs account: the charge would begin 'He answers for 5 pigs remaining and for 7 remaining as piglets on the last account', and the piglets account would cover only those born or bought during the current year. Often it was done more elaborately: the piglets account would begin 'He answers for 7 remaining' and its discharge section would include the entry 'Added to the pigs, 7', while the charge section of the pigs account would say 'Added from the piglets, 7'. We thus find the same seven piglets occurring in more than one paragraph of the account. This could well become quite complicated. It became normal to have separate accounts for calves, for year-old cattle, for two-year olds and for each of the three classes of adult, bulls, cows and oxen. A calf born on the manor and kept there would thus join the appropriate class of adult stock only on its third successive annual transfer in the accounts. The same system of moving items from one paragraph to another of the same account might be applied to other things besides livestock: we quite often, for instance, find quantities of corn being transferred, by entries in the discharge section of the accounts for, say, barley and oats, to an account for the mixed corn which was used to pay the wages of the manorial servants. All of which is a good deal simpler in practice than it may sound. Probably the best introduction to the workings of the manorial account is to compare accounts from two or more successive years from some fairly straightforward published series, such as those from Sevenhampton (Wiltshire) for 1275–88 or from Cuxham (Oxfordshire) for 1288–99 (see the select texts listed at the end of this chapter).

It must already be clear that the annual account for a single manor may contain an enormous amount of detailed information; and that this information is presented in such a way that the entire account is directed to the single aim of establishing the state of affairs between the local official and his lord – how much was owed in cash, and what remained on the manor in corn, livestock and other goods at the end of the accounting year. To show what profits the manor had brought the lord in the course of the year was no part of the account's ostensible purpose; we have seen how it brackets together in the cash discharge both the running costs of the manor and the money that was handed over to the lord from the year's takings. At the same time the account unquestionably gives enough information for the manor's profitability to be worked out, and it is clear that manorial accounts were used for this from a very early date. The earliest of the general audit (assisa scaccarii) rolls from Canterbury Cathedral Priory in 1225 concludes the summary account of each manor in demesne with the amount of profit, and there is a note of the profit on the earliest of any surviving accounts for an individual manor, for Froyle (Hampshire) in about 1233.[9] It may well be that one reason why written accounts came into use was that manorial profits could be calculated from them, something that could not be done if accounts were presented orally. These profits would be the lord's net gain from the manor each year, taking into account the running costs and the value of produce delivered to his household, and sometimes distinguishing between the profits of demesne agriculture and the profits of the manor overall. Dr E. Stone, in a study of great

⁹ D. & C. Canterbury, Assisa Scaccarii Roll 1; B.L. Add. Roll 17468.

interest, has shown that on the Norwich Cathedral Priory estates the figures for profit were reached by calculations of some subtlety and that in the early fourteenth century these figures were being used to decide whether to lease manors out or keep them in demesne.[10] It is not often that we can reconstruct the calculations of profit, even where we have the final figure that was reached; there are normally too many imponderables in the way of allowances for produce sent to the lord's household or for items bought on the manor for use elsewhere, or even for depreciation of stock. But, however the figure was arrived at, it can be of great interest to know how much profit a manor's lord believed that it brought him in the course of the year. Only a minority of surviving manorial accounts enter the amount of profit, but it is a substantial minority, and the information can easily be overlooked, partly because it may be entered at the extreme end of the cash account, often well beyond the rest of the writing, partly because of the variety of words used for profit: *clarum, comodum, valor, waynagium,* as well as the more obvious *profectus* or *proficuum.*

Phase 1

The first phase of manorial accounts covers those from the first half of the thirteenth century, when few estates used accounts, along with later accounts on some estates where the characteristic early forms were only slowly superseded. Its most striking feature is that the accounts were produced by the estate's central organisation. Often what we have are enrolled accounts for all its manors, whether compiled at a single operation (as at Peterborough Abbey) or a few manors at a time as the audit proceeded (as on the Bec Abbey estates).[11] By far the most notable series of these enrolled accounts is from the bishop of Winchester's estates (see Plate 4); they survive for most years from 1208–9 down to 1611 (in books, not rolls, from the mid fifteenth century onwards), a historical source of great importance which has already been extensively used but which still has much more to reveal.[12] On at least two estates early enrolled accounts give way to separate accounts for individual manors, perhaps developed from the draft accounts that must have been used to compile the enrolments: at Winchester Cathedral Priory probably in the 1250s, at Crowland Abbey (Lincolnshire) between 1315 and 1319.[13] But the individual accounts, just like the enrolments, were compiled by the estate's central administration and record the state of affairs as agreed at the end of the audit.

It is important to bear this in mind when using Phase 1 accounts: they are agreed accounts, agreed that is to the satisfaction of the lord of the manor. The expenses they record, for instance, may not be the actual amounts spent, but simply the amounts the lord was prepared to allow to his official. In accounts of Phase 2 we get a far closer insight into the process of auditing and we see the

[10] E. Stone, 'Profit-and-loss Accountancy at Norwich Cathedral Priory', *T.R.H.S.* 5th Ser. xii (1962), pp.25–48.

[11] Peterborough: Northants. Record Office, Fitzwilliam (Milton) MSS. 233, 2388, 2389 (accounts of 1301–2, 1309–11), and others. Bec: muniments of King's College, Cambridge, Ministers' accounts before the time of the College (accounts of 1283–4).

[12] Hampshire Record Office, Eccles. 2/159270–159444, 155827–155942.

[13] After the enrolled accounts of (respectively) 1247–8, 1314–15, the next accounts to survive are for single manors (Alton Priors, etc., 1260–1; Oakington, 1319–20) which demonstrably were once in annual files each covering the whole estate (D. & C. Winchester; muniments of Queens' College, Cambridge, now deposited in Cambridge University Library).

year's transactions from the viewpoint of the local official as well as of the lord; accounts of Phase 1 show us the viewpoint of the lord alone.

However, what we do occasionally see in manorial accounts of Phase 1, and in no others, is the close association of manorial and household accounts. The general audit rolls of Canterbury Cathedral Priory from the 1220s onwards include accounts of the sacrist, cellarer and other non-manorial officers; at Peterborough Abbey in the early fourteenth century, accounts of the pig-keeper and the bakery were enrolled along with the manorial accounts.[14] Half of the specimen accounts from Beaulieu Abbey in 1269–70 are for officers and other workers around the monastery itself, not on the estates. All this is a useful reminder that manorial accounts give only half the financial picture; they show us the income-producing side of the organisation of which the other half, the expending side, was the household. It is dangerously easy for the manorial historian to forget that this other side of his finances was of no less importance to the solvency of the medieval lord, whether lay, episcopal or monastic.

One characteristic of Phase 1 accounts is a certain variety between one estate and another. This may be in purely external features. Thus the enrolled accounts from the Bec Abbey estates put the cash accounts for all the manors on the front of the roll, the corn accounts on the dorse, instead of (as in enrolled accounts elsewhere) placing the corn account for each manor immediately after its cash account. But variations also occur in the internal arrangements of the account. A very persistent example is in accounts from estates centred on the Winchester area and also, interestingly, in those from Peterborough Abbey. Here, as elsewhere, the amounts due from tenants' rents were one of the first items in the charge section of the cash account; but they were then followed by entries of rents that could not be collected for one reason or another (from a vacant holding, for instance, or where the tenant was excused payment through working as a manorial servant), and a balance was drawn to show the net receipts from rents as the effective amount the official was to answer for. On other estates these missing rents (defects of rent: *defectus reddituum*) would form an entirely separate entry in the discharge section of the account. The final balance of the account would be the same, but it would be reached by a slightly different route.

Whatever the minor variations in Phase 1 accounts, they all reflect the contemporary pattern of estate management. This was the early period of demesne farming, when a hierarchy of supervisors kept watch on all the doings of the local officials (above, pp.5–6). On some estates (as those of the archbishop of Canterbury or of both the bishop and the cathedral priory at Winchester) accounts were presented jointly by both the manor's own reeve and the bailiff who had oversight of two or three manors, and they thus begin 'A. reeve and B. bailiff render account . . .';[15] but in the final balance the verb is in the singular – 'And he owes . . .' (*Et debet . . .*) – because it was the reeve alone who carried the financial responsibility. There was a general tendency not to leave money in the reeve's hands: the lord's representative would come to collect the proceeds soon after each quarter-day when the tenants paid rent, and both cash and corn

---

[14] D. & C. Canterbury, Assisa Scaccarii rolls; Northants. Record Office, Fitzwilliam (Milton) MSS. 233, 2388, 2389.

[15] J.S Drew, 'Manorial Accounts of St. Swithun's Priory, Winchester', *E.H.R.* lxii (1947), pp.26–7; *Winch. Pipe Roll 1210–11*, p.xx; cf. for the archbishopric of Canterbury B.L. Add. MS. 29794.

accounts were often closed at the end of the year so that no corn would be left in the granary and no money owing would be carried forward into the next year's account. It may have been to make this easier that Ramsey Abbey had an accounting year that ended at Michaelmas (29 September) for cash but at Lammas (1 August) for corn.[16]

Particularly interesting in Phase 1 accounts are the changes we see in the course of time, changes that nearly always tended towards greater detail and greater uniformity. Livestock, for instance, came normally to be included in a manorial account instead of often being either omitted altogether (as on the Bec Abbey estates) or covered by a simple inventory (as at Crowland Abbey). More and more detail was included in the cash accounts, which rapidly developed a system of subdivisions. In many of the earliest accounts, the cash is entered simply in two paragraphs, one for the charge, one for the discharge, though particular items might be distinguished with a special marginal heading (as the bishopric of Winchester always did for the profits of manorial courts: *purchasia*). As time went on more and more items would be hived off into special paragraphs of this sort, so that eventually both charge and discharge sections consisted of a whole series of separate paragraphs, each with its own heading and total. In each of the two sections there would be a hard core of miscellaneous items that could not be hived off in this way, each forming a paragraph on its own with a heading that had once belonged to the entire section: issues of the manor (*exitus manerii*), formerly the whole charge section, were now simply the miscellaneous receipts, necessary expenses (*expense necessarie*), formerly the whole discharge, were now the petty expenses alone.[17] Other changes tended towards rationalisation. Instead of, for example, having separate paragraphs for corn that came from multure (toll from mills) or for chickens received from the rent known as churchscot, these would be included in the general paragraphs for the appropriate type of corn or poultry. An ever more rigorous logic was applied to the account – to the division between charge and discharge and to the classification of the various items of account.

Phase 2
We can thus see developing in the first phase of manorial accounting the uniformity that is one of the features of Phase 2. This uniformity is the more striking in view of the rapid proliferation of manorial accounts: Phase 2 broadly covers the hundred years from the mid or late thirteenth century, when written accounts became an almost universal feature of English estate management. Yet everywhere – whether the estate was large or small, whether it was lay or ecclesiastical, whether its centre was at one end of the country or the other – these accounts closely follow a single pattern, both in external form and in the methods of accountancy. The account will be for a single manor. On the inside, or front, of the roll is the cash account, divided into its many paragraphs, and on the outside, or dorse, are the accounts for the various types first of corn and then of stock. There were conventions, closely observed, about the order of items within this framework. Thus the cash charge always begins with arrears carried forward from the previous account, followed by the tenants' rents; in the cash discharge

[16] B.L. Add. Roll 39669.

[17] In successive accounts between c.1233 and 1263 from Froyle (Hants.), a manor of St Mary's Abbey, Winchester, we can clearly see this process occurring (B.L. Add. Rolls 13338, 13339, 17457–17478; Hampshire Record Office, Winchester City records L1/1/1).

CASH CHARGE
   Arrears
   Assessed rents
   Rents of mills
   Sale of corn
   Sale of malt
   Sale of stock
   Issues of the manor
   Sale of cheese
   Profits of the court
   Forinsec receipts
   Sales at the audit
     (*Vendicio super compotum*)

CASH DISCHARGE
   Allowances of rent
   Costs of ploughs
   Costs of carts
   Necessary expenses
   Costs of mills
   Purchase of corn
   Purchase of stock
   Costs of mowing, hoeing
   Harvest expenses
   Labourers' wages
   Lord's expenses
   Visitors' expenses
   Forinsec expenses

CORN
   Wheat
   Small-corn of wheat
   Barley
   Dredge
   White peas
   Grey peas
   Vetch
   Oats
   Malt of wheat
   Other malt
   Mixed corn for wages

STOCK
   Cart-horses
   Plough-horses
   Bulls
   Oxen
   Cows
   Bullocks
   Heifers
   2-year old cattle
   1-year old cattle
   Calves
   Rams
   Wethers
   Ewes
   2-year old wethers
   2-year old ewes
   1-year old sheep
   Lambs
   Pigs
   Piglets
   Geese
   Capons
   Cocks and hens
   Chicks
   Ducks
   Eggs
   Doves
   Sides of bacon
   Cheese
   Milk
   Hides
   Wool
   Lambs' wool
   Woolfells

LABOUR SERVICES
   Winter ploughworks
   Autumn ploughworks
   Harvest works
   Carrying services
   Miscellaneous winter works
   Miscellaneous summer works

Figure 3. Headings of a typical early-fourteenth-century manorial account.

the paragraphs for the running costs of ploughs and carts are always near the beginning; the corn accounts always deal with wheat, rye, barley and oats in that order; and in the livestock accounts horses are always entered before cattle, cattle before sheep. Where a manorial account of Phase 2 differs from the standard form, this nearly always reflects some peculiarity of the manor itself – it might be purely a dairy-farm, for instance, or a group of rent-paying town houses – not a variation in accounting style peculiar to a particular region or estate. This uniformity, together with the division of the whole account into headed paragraphs, is extremely helpful to the historian who, with a little experience, can often find the information he needs from no more than a moment's glance, even though the account itself may be long and complex. Some idea of the length and detail of an early-fourteenth-century account is given by Figure 3, which sets out a typical list of paragraph headings.

    Despite this uniformity, another characteristic of Phase 2 accounts is that they were locally produced. Instead of enrolled accounts or accounts for individual manors written up after the audit by the estate's central administration, what we have are accounts written for the local officials before the audit by clerks of their own choosing. The account would be presented at the audit as the basis of the official's claim; often his clerk would be there to help him make his case. Any changes imposed by the auditors would be entered on the account, sometimes by the local clerk but more often by the auditors' own clerk, and the auditors would then take the account to be kept in the estate's central records; further small additions might be made to it, such as a note of the manor's profit for the year. This means that a Phase 2 account shows what happened at the audit; we see what the local official claimed, what was queried or disallowed by the auditors and very often why, for revealing notes and comments may be added to explain the alterations made on the account – 'In future so much will not be allowed', 'In future the number of acres of each sort of corn should be entered' (in the costs of reaping), 'This has been sworn to at the audit', and so on. It is usually quite easy to tell what was originally written on the account and what was added at the audit; even when the local clerk entered the auditors' alterations so that they are in the same hand as the rest, the difference in ink or simply what is written makes it clear what are the additions. The result is that a Phase 2 account is virtually a dialogue, a debate between local official and auditors, not a statement from a single viewpoint like a Phase 1 account. This adds greatly to its interest and historical value.

When the account was first drawn up the clerk would normally leave blanks in the cash account for the individual paragraph totals and for the grand totals of charge and discharge and the final balance; sometimes he entered provisional figures as a guide to the auditors, but they would be written very small to one side or even with a system of dots instead of normal figures. This meant that the auditors could alter the cash account without difficulty: they could add or increase entries of amounts received, or they could strike out or reduce the amounts claimed as expenses, all without having to cross out and rewrite totals already written in. It was otherwise on the dorse, in the corn and stock accounts. Here the totals and balances remaining could hardly be changed on audit for they recorded the actual state of affairs on the manor: the amount of barley remaining in the granary, the number of lambs in the fold, of hens in the yard, and so on. Accordingly they were fully filled in on the account when it was first written out, before the audit. If the auditors refused to pass any entry on the corn or stock account they would cross it out or alter it just as on the cash account, but because the balance remaining could not be changed they would add an extra entry to the relevant discharge paragraph, recording a sale 'at the audit' (*super compotum*) corresponding to what had been disallowed. If, say, the account claimed that 4 quarters 7 bushels of oats had been sown as seed and the auditors held that 4 quarters was the most that should have been used, the entry in the oats discharge would be altered and a further entry of 7 bushels 'sold at the audit' added at the end of the paragraph; there would be no need to change the paragraph total or balance. At the same time the auditors would usually put a 3-shaped sign in the margin opposite their 'sold at the audit' entry; when they had finished going through the corn and stock accounts it was easy to spot all these entries of fictitious sales, and a new paragraph of 'Sales at the audit' (*Vendiciones super compotum*) would be added to the cash charge on the front of the roll so that the value of all these disallowed items of corn and stock would be charged against the official as part of the cash reckoning (see Plate 5). This, again, is much more easily seen in operation than described; study of an original Phase 2 account on which the entries made by the auditors' clerk can be clearly distinguished will show very simply how the system of fictitious sales worked. It does not appear on the earliest Phase 2 accounts, but was in general use by the early fourteenth century. It was not understood by historians until J.S Drew's exposition in 1947 from the accounts of Winchester Cathedral Priory.[18]

From these same accounts Drew described another sort of entry that is widely found, the entry of minimum or fixed returns (*responsiones*) for particular items of corn or livestock.[19] In some Phase 2 accounts (not, usually, before the fourteenth century) we find a marginal note added at the audit beside the account for each type of corn to show how the yield from the harvest compared with the amount of seed sown: 'He returns a fourfold yield, but for 3 bushels' (*Respondet ad quartum granum minus iii bussellos*) for instance. At first these entries seem to have been simply for information, recording the actual yield achieved, but soon they were being used to extract a minimum yield: if the actual yield fell below what was required or expected an entry for the missing amount would be added to the charge paragraph of the account for that type of corn 'so that he may return a fourfold yield' (*ut respondeat ad quartum granum*), and another entry would be added to the discharge paragraph recording the same amount as a fictitious sale, a sale at the audit, to be charged against the official on the cash account. The same system would be applied to livestock if the number of eggs per hen or the number of piglets per sow was thought insufficient. Eventually on some estates the required minimum yield became a fixed yield: provided the official answered for this predetermined amount, any extra he achieved by good luck or good management was his to keep, so that year after year we find on the accounts precisely the same return for particular items of corn or livestock.[20] The accounts have, in fact, ceased to record actual manorial production; yet there is nothing on the individual account to show this, and we can discover what has happened only if we see the accounts for a whole series of years. The historian forgets at his peril that the purpose of a manorial account was to establish the state of reckoning between lord and local official: we should never take for granted that it records what really happened on the manor.

Here we see changes in the manorial account reflecting changes in estate management: the predetermined fixed yield for corn or livestock was a first step towards leasing the entire manor, replacing the local official, the reeve or bailiff, with a lessee farmer. Other changes in manorial accounts in the course of Phase 2 continued the developments of the first phase: accounts became ever longer and fuller as the hierarchy of supervisors to watch the local official was replaced by ever more detailed and searching scrutiny at the audit. Throughout the account more and more information is given: the number of acres sown with each type of corn for instance, or the actual dates when corn was sold at a particular price. Often the trend is most obvious in the stock account: further paragraphs provide

[18] Drew, op. cit., p.30.

[19] Drew, op. cit., p.41. But the significance of the simple notes of yield was known earlier – e.g. Frances G. Davenport, *The Economic Development of a Norfolk Manor 1086–1565* (Cambridge, 1906), pp.29–31.

[20] Winchester Cathedral Priory went even further and nearly every manor that kept pigs, geese, or hens accounted for 60 piglets, 28 goslings, 60 chicks and 300 eggs as each year's issue, irrespective of the number of adult stock of the manor (Drew, op. cit., p.39).

a formal account of an increasing range of live and dead stock – hay, turves, hurdles, peacocks' feathers, roof-tiles, brass bowls and table-cloths are only examples of the enormous variety of items separately accounted for on one or other manor in the mid fourteenth century. There could be further additions. Sometimes we find a works account, its charge being the labour services due on the demesne and its discharge showing how they were used; we even find the fictitious sale being used to charge the reeve for works that had not been performed. Sometimes there are separate accounts for week-works, harvest works and other types of service. And very occasionally there is a land account, showing how the demesne arable and meadows had been used during the year.[21]

When a new reeve or bailiff took office one would expect him to start with a clean slate, so that the only debts he owed on his first account were those incurred in the single year's business. But it became increasingly common for the lord of the manor to saddle him with any outstanding debts of his predecessor, so that his first account could open with an entry of arrears. This meant only that it was the new official's job to collect the money that was owing; the lord and his auditors did not lose sight of who the real debtor was, and at the end of the account there will commonly be a note to say how much was due from the present official, how much from his predecessor. Where an office changed hands frequently this note might divide the debt between several successive holders. This method of bringing forward the former officials' debts had become the general practice by the time the third phase of manorial accounting began.[22]

Phase 3

Phase 3 of manorial accounting belongs to the period, from the mid fourteenth century onwards, when leasing manors was becoming once again the usual way of running an estate, and its most characteristic features result directly from this change. Above all, the uniformity that marked the second phase disappeared. Where a manor continued to be run in demesne, its accounts followed the same pattern as before. But when it was leased there was bound to be a change. The lessee farmer might present an annual written account just as the reeve or bailiff had done (in fact he seems normally to have done so) but he had much less to account to the landlord for: normally no corn or livestock, no money apart from the amount of his annual farm and no expenses beyond perhaps some building repairs. The result might be a very short document indeed – short and relatively uninformative, as the landlord and his auditors had ceased to take an interest in the minute detail that gives the accounts of manors in demesne such great historical value. Sometimes, indeed, the farmer's account was not only short but scrappy and informal; some cover more than one year.[23] But often it retained the formal structure of a Phase 2 account, simply adapted to serve for a lessee farmer. One reason for this variety was the lack of any generally accepted form or models for the clerks who drew up lessees' accounts; we have specimen accounts from the fifteenth century, but they are simply copies of the form used for manors in demesne,[24] and how this was adapted for manors at farm was entirely a matter of

---

[21] As at Oakington (Cambs.) in 1361–2 (Page, *Crowland*, p.279).

[22] It can be seen in operation in successive collectors' accounts at Oakington from 1347 to 1351 (Page, *Crowland*, pp.266–71).

[23] e.g. farmers' accounts for Cuxham (Oxon.) from 1395 on, in the muniments of Merton College, Oxford, 5888–5897.

[24] *Henley*, pp.247, 249–52.

individual choice or local tradition. But besides this the many different forms and conditions of manorial leases were bound to produce greater variety of manorial account than in Phase 2, just because there was greater variety between one manor and another in what had to be accounted for.

Nor was it only the lessee who rendered account when a manor was set to farm. As we have seen, the lord normally excluded from the lease at least the rents of the local tenants and the profits of the manorial court, and he would appoint a collector on the manor to gather them in for him. This collector would render an annual account, so that we may have two separate accounts each year from the same manor. Sometimes the farmer and the collector presented a single joint account.[25] Occasionally a collector was appointed even when demesne farming was continued or (as could happen) restored on a particular manor; in this case the reeve or bailiff accounted for everything that would be leased if the manor were set to farm, the collector for everything else.[26] A further complication arises in nomenclature: the lessee was sometimes referred to not as farmer but as reeve or bailiff, as though he were the local official in charge of a manor in demesne. The significance of a Phase 3 account – just who is accounting for what – can be understood only by approaching it with an open, flexible mind; it is far harder than with earlier manorial accounts to know what to expect from a simple catalogue entry or description.

Despite all the variety of form and content, the basic structure of a charge-discharge account remained, but we see continuing developments in its detailed layout. These particularly affected the end of the cash account (and the cash account was, of course, normally the entire account when the manor was at farm). We find in accounts of Phase 2 that after the auditors had completed their work and entered the final balance the official would successfully plead against particular disallowances they had made, and a note of this would be added with a new balance. Sometimes this process would be formalised by setting out a special paragraph of 'Petitions for allowance' (*Petitiones allocancie*) after the first balance. In Phase 3 accounts we find this developed still further, with the first balance followed by very long notes, usually set out with the first line rather short, starting quite close to the right-hand edge of the membrane, then with each successive line starting further out to the left, producing a nearly triangular pattern (see Plate 6). Several successive new balances might be struck, and in a short account of a lessee or collector these notes may well be longer than everything preceding them. It seems as if it was after the audit had produced its first formal balance that the real business of investigation and discussion began. It meant that a substantial part of the account lay outside the formal structure, marking a further move towards variety, away from the uniformity of the Phase 2 account.

Sometimes, like some other late-medieval records, the manorial account became over-formalised, so that its layout and contents owed more to precedent than to current fact. Thus the traditional pattern might be adhered to so far that the account for a manor at farm included headings that could apply only if it were in demesne, 'Nothing' (*Nichil*) being entered after each.[27] Or within the

---

[25] As at Urchfont (Wilts.) in 1463–4, where the stock-keeper also shared the account (B.L. Add. Roll 66603). Sometimes farmer and collector were the same person, as at Down Hatherley (Gloucs.) in 1464–5 (B.L. Add. Charter 74143).

[26] As at Oakington in 1361–2 (Page, *Crowland*, pp.271–9: reeve's account).

[27] As at Reedham (Norf.) in 1444–5 (B.L. Add. Roll 26863).

individual paragraphs items might be included because they appeared on previous accounts or a rental, even though this year there was nothing to enter against them. Thus on the account for the countess of Devon's manor of Tiverton in 1511–12 the paragraph of minor receipts contains twenty-four items of which all but four are negative ones: 'Of certain items there nothing has been sold this year by the said accounting official. He does not answer for old oaks or cropping of oaks . . .' and so on.[28] This formalisation may be carried to the point where it is not just quaint but misleading. Mr T.B. Pugh shows how in accounts for Stow, near Newport (Monmouthshire), we find the mistress (*concubina*) of Master William Cady, who was himself alive in 1424, paying 2*s.* a year for a cottage and one acre in 1446 – and still in 1522. The name of the tenant would be entered on the account from the latest rental, which by then was a hundred years out of date.[29] We must always be on our guard against this sort of quirk; as Dr C. Dyer has put it, 'Reading fifteenth-century manorial accounts is an exercise in distinguishing between theory and reality'.[30]

Most of our manorial accounts of Phase 3 were drawn up locally to present to the audit, and like Phase 2 accounts they show us the auditors' alterations and comments. But more often than in the second phase we find accounts that are obvious fair copies made after audit,[31] and it is not uncommon in the late middle ages to find manorial accounts for an entire estate enrolled after audit as a record for its central administration.[32] On a few estates, like the bishop of Winchester's, we know that this represents a long-continued tradition from the first phase of manorial accounting, and on other estates too it may be mere chance that has preserved only late survivors of lengthy series. But the pattern of survival suggests strongly that in some cases at least we have a reversion to the practice of enrolment which many estates had abandoned in the late thirteenth or early fourteenth century.

The central organisation: receivers' accounts and valors
Throughout this chapter we have been discussing manorial accounts from the viewpoint of the user, the historian. We have been looking at the details of the year's financial transactions on the individual manor, the reckoning of account between the manorial lord and the man on the spot – whether reeve or farmer, official or lessee – wherever we could find them: in accounts drawn up before audit, in fair copies made afterwards, in enrolments made by the estate's central administration. We have seen that they conform to a single pattern of arrangement, which develops and changes over the years but which is common to original draft, fair copy and enrolment alike. But it is important to bear in mind that to the medieval estate administrator – and thus to the archivist – what we have lumped together in this way as 'manorial accounts' comprised several different sorts of document, which will have played a variety of roles in the organisations that brought them into being. In comparing the locally produced

[28] B.L. Add. Roll 64823.
[29] *Marcher Lordships*, p.162.
[30] C. Dyer, *Lords and Peasants in a Changing Society: the Estates of the Bishopric of Worcester, 680–1540* (Cambridge, 1980), p.162.
[31] As at Ashey (I. of Wight) in 1535–6 (B.L. Add. Roll 74601).
[32] To take two examples on different scales, the enrolled estate accounts from Taunton Priory in 1437–9 (B.L. Add. Rolls 16333, 25873) and from the bishopric of Lincoln in 1509–10 (Lincolnshire Archives Office, diocesan records, B.P. accounts 8).

accounts of Phase 2 with the centrally enrolled accounts of Phase 1 we are not, archivally speaking, comparing like with like. The financial transactions of the individual manor will often have acquired the permanence of the written word at some higher level of the estate organisation.

On a large medieval estate there were generally three levels of financial responsibility: the manorial official or lessee, the local receiver who collected money from the manors in a particular area, and the receiver-general who channelled the money from the local receivers to the lord and his household. Smaller estates would have a simpler organisation, and in any case there was some variety in the officials' titles, in the division of responsibilities and in the detailed administrative machinery – all of which affected the style of the accounts presented at each level. What part was played in this supra-manorial structure by the varying forms of manorial account – original draft, fair copy or enrolment – is often far from clear, and probably differed significantly from one estate to another. There have been quite a number of studies of the financial structure of particular medieval estates,[33] but still more knowledge here would assist our full understanding of the records and of the information we draw from them. From a number of estates in the fourteenth and fifteenth centuries we have substantial series of receivers' accounts, accounts which give us no more than summaries of the receipts from individual manors. Mr T.B. Pugh's edition of the individual manorial accounts and receiver's account for the duke of Buckingham's lordship of Newport in 1447–8 displays very clearly the typical relationship between the two levels of account in the late middle ages (see the select texts listed at the end of this chapter).[34]

However summary the details on a receiver's account, it may provide useful information about the individual manors if manorial accounts are lacking. So too may the valor. This sets out the income and expenses of an estate in more or less summary form but sometimes showing how much each manor could be expected to provide each year. A detailed valor will tell us a good deal about what was happening on each manor, with its entries for the leases of mills, hiring out of pasture, sales of timber, losses of rent for want of tenants and so on. The valor was not an account – indeed it might be seen as a form of survey – but it was based directly on the manorial and receivers' accounts and some lords had one compiled every year as a current guide to their financial resources. The formal valor first appears in the second half of the fourteenth century, but it can be compared with the summarised accounts for an entire estate that we sometimes find in the thirteenth century, and, indeed, with enrolled or filed copies of manorial accounts, which may well have served the same purpose.

Subsidiary records of account

We now pass from the highest level of the estate's financial administration to the lowest, to the ephemeral records that were used in drawing up the manorial account. They must usually have been thrown away once their immediate purpose was served but occasionally we find some kept along with the accounts

---

[33] Most recently P.H.W. Booth, *The Financial Administration of the Lordship and County of Chester 1272–1377*, Chetham Soc. 3rd Ser. xxviii (1981).

[34] P.R.O. DL29/354/5837 is an unpublished file of six local accounts and one receiver's account for the duchy of Lancaster's barony of Embleton (Northumb.), 1367–8, which likewise demonstrates both simply and neatly the relationship between the two levels of account.

themselves. They must have varied to some extent from one estate to another; all we can do here is to mention briefly those most likely to be encountered.

Draft accounts of some sort must have been used to compile all the enrolled accounts of Phase 1, though we hardly ever have both the original and the enrolment. Here, of course, calling the original a draft may be open to question: the individual accounts which were used to compile the enrolments for the bishopric of Winchester and which survive in substantial series from the mid fourteenth century on are carefully written accounts of Phase 2 pattern. But we occasionally find that a Phase 2 account exists in both draft and fair copy; the draft will often give slightly more detail than the fair copy, it may show signs of having been drawn up in successive stages in the course of the year, and, in consequence, the contents of each paragraph may be less well ordered.

Views of account sometimes served as draft accounts. The view was an inspection of the financial state of the manor made by the auditors about halfway through the year. We find so few references to these views in manorial records that we may wonder whether they really were made as regularly as was urged by the thirteenth-century treatises on estate management. When they were held, they may often have been conducted orally without a written record; but sometimes the current state of account was written out in a document that has survived. At its most formal, the view of account is a short version of the full annual account and it may show the same process of auditing; it may even contain fictitious sales ('sold at the view': *in vendicione super visum*).[35]

Particulars of account normally survive only if they are physically attached to the account itself. Often no more than tiny scraps of parchment or paper, they set out the full details of items (usually among the cash expenses) that are entered in the account only as a single total; this was information which the auditors might call for but which would overweight the relevant paragraph if put in the account itself. Expenses over the harvest period, lists of tenants and their rents, costs of putting up a new building, are among the many items that might be covered in this way.

Lists of estreats were certainly a normal part of manorial administration but have very seldom survived. They are the lists of fines and amercements imposed in the manorial court (see below, p.50), and would be given to the local official so that he could collect the money from the people concerned. Where they have been attached to an account they presumably served as particulars of account for the profits of the court.[36]

Indentures with the local official were also very common; a simple note in two parts, indented along the division, often took the place of a wooden tally-stick as a receipt or voucher that he would keep as evidence of a particular payment or delivery of produce. Occasionally indentures of this sort survive by serving as particulars of account, but mostly, like the tallies, they would be thrown away once they had been produced and checked at the audit. More formal indentures survive more often, but may not have been so much a part of normal practice. Among them are indentures of account, drawn up at the end of the audit and listing the cash debts, corn and livestock that the official took over at the start of the new financial year; and indentures, similarly listing the manorial stock, that

[35] As at Syleham (Suff.) in 1273–4 (P.R.O. SC6/751/7).
[36] As at Maidstone (Kent) in 1296–7, 1299–1300 (Lambeth Palace Library, London, estate documents, rolls 657, 658).

would be drawn up between a new local official and either his predecessor or the lord of the manor.

Select texts

Titow, *Rural Soc.* pp.106–36. Phase 1 and Phase 2 enrolled accounts for Downton (Wilts.), 1208–9 and 1324–5. English translation.

Winch. Pipe Roll 1210–11. Phase 1 enrolled accounts. Latin text.

Page, *Crowland*, pp.174–279. Phase 1 enrolled accounts for the whole estate, 1258–9, and select accounts for Cottenham, Dry Drayton and Oakington (Cambs.), 1267–1362, showing development from Phase 1 through Phase 2 to Phase 3. Latin text.

Stratton Accts. pp.31–233. Phase 2 accounts, with drafts, view and particulars of account for Sevenhampton (Wilts.), 1269–88. Latin text.

Cuxham Man. Recs. pp.117–606. Phase 2 accounts, 1276, 1288–99, 1317–19, 1327–30, 1346–59, and subsidiary records of accounts, 1272–1355. Latin text.

Ministers' Accounts of the Manor of Petworth 1347–1353, ed. L.F. Salzman, Sussex Record Soc. lv (1955). Phase 2 accounts. English translation.

N.W. Alcock, 'An East Devon Manor in the Later Middle Ages', *Report and Transactions of the Devonshire Association*, cii (1970), pp.176–85; cv (1973), pp.178–90. Phase 2 account, 1398–9, and Phase 3 accounts, 1428–9 and (in three versions) 1524–5. Latin text.

Marcher Lordships, pp.184–236. Phase 3 accounts, with receiver's account and summarised 'declaration of account' and valor, for the manors, etc., of the lordship of Newport (Monm.), 1447–8. Latin or (for the declaration of account) original English text.

Ruthin Valor. Valor of the English lands of the earl of Kent from accounts of 1467–8. Original English text.

Percy Bailiffs' Rolls of the Fifteenth Century, ed. J.C. Hodgson, Surtees Soc. cxxxiv (1921). Phase 3 enrolled accounts for the earldom of Northumberland, 1471–2. Latin text.

Bolton Rentals, pp.25–61. Accounts of local officials, based on rentals, 1538–9. English translation.

Further reading

An important pioneer work based on manorial records that discusses helpfully the detailed contents of the various paragraphs of the manorial account is by A. Elizabeth Levett, 'The Black Death on the Estates of the See of Winchester', in *Oxf. Studies*, v (1916), pp.13–67. N. Denholm–Young, *Seignorial Administration in England* (London, 1937), looking at thirteenth-century lay estates, clearly shows the place of manorial accounts and audit in the overall organisation of estate and household. Two later studies that are basic to our understanding of the use and purpose of manorial accounts are J.S. Drew, 'Manorial Accounts of St. Swithun's Priory, Winchester', *E.H.R.* lxii (1947), pp.20–41, and E. Stone, 'Profit-and-loss Accountancy at Norwich Cathedral Priory', *T.R.H.S.* 5th Ser. xii (1962), pp.25–48. A detailed discussion of the development of Phase 2 accounts, of how they were drawn up and of the subsidiary accounting records that were used, is in the introduction of *Cuxham Man. Recs.* pp.12–71, while *Marcher Lordships*, pp.153–83, provides an important discussion of the local accounts, receivers' accounts and valors of the lordship of Newport (Monm.) in the fifteenth century, an analysis that is of general relevance to late-medieval manorial and other estate accounts. A more general discussion of receivers' accounts and valors is in C.D Ross and T.B. Pugh, 'Materials for the Study of Baronial Incomes in Fifteenth-century England', *Economic History Review*, 2nd Ser. vi (1953–4), pp.190–4; valors are also discussed in the introduction to *Ruthin Valor*, pp.8–9. Treatises on manorial accounting (including the anonymous treatise on husbandry, which originated in auditors' rules) are fully listed and discussed, and some texts printed, by Dorothea Oschinsky in *Henley*, pp.200–57, 417–75.

CHAPTER IV

COURT RECORDS

Origin and composition

Our earliest records of manorial courts are on some of our earliest manorial accounts. The enrolled accounts of the bishopric of Winchester, which first survive from 1208–9, give among the cash receipts for each manor a detailed list of all the fines and amercements imposed by the manorial court: 2*s*. from Wigain as an entry fine, 6*d*. from Walter de Harinegate for permission to lease out land, 6*d*. from Widow Wrenc for default in harvest works, 6*d*. from William Walense for brawling, and so on.[1] Most later series of manorial accounts enter the profits of the court as a single lump sum, and we may assume that the early Winchester accounts gave these details because there were then no court rolls on which the full proceedings of the manorial courts would be recorded. This accords with the pattern of surviving court rolls. We have extracts from court rolls of St. Albans Abbey manors from 1237 on, and a Ramsey Abbey cartulary contains a copy of a court roll of 1239–40, but our earliest original court roll is for the English manors of Bec Abbey and dates from 1246.[2] It is only from the 1270s onwards that we have manorial court rolls in anything like profusion, and this probably reflects the spread of the idea of keeping a formal record of the courts' proceedings. Unlike the entries from manorial courts on the Winchester account rolls, the court roll was not primarily a financial record – it contains far too much information that is irrelevant to finance. As R.B. Pugh put it, referring to the court rolls of Adam de Stratton's Wiltshire manors, 'the leading motive for writing out these and similar court rolls was to ensure that justice was done according to precedent'.[3] Nor, of course, was it primarily for financial reasons that manorial courts were held; it is not uncommon to find that the profits were minimal, as at Little Hormead (Hertfordshire) in about 1260, when the court's total proceeds were 3*s*. 0*d*., the steward's expenses in holding it 2*s*. 8*d*., or even non-existent, as at Thanington (Kent) where in 1443 the court was said to be worth nothing once the steward's fee had been paid.[4]

Precedent was all-important in the manorial court as in other medieval courts of law. The early extracts from the court rolls of St Albans Abbey are in books that were drawn up, one for each manor, from the mid fourteenth century onwards; they contain copies of all entries in the rolls that were thought to be useful for future reference. We have similar compilations from other estates, usually bringing together some particular type of information from a mass of individual court rolls – for instance the series of 50-foot long rolls, one for each manor, on which the cellarer of Waltham Abbey in about 1538 listed references to tenants taking over or giving up holdings since the late fifteenth century.[5] On the other hand, to find a manorial court roll copied into a cartulary, as we have

---

[1] *Winch. Pipe Roll 1210–11*, p.113
[2] Levett, *Studies*, pp.79–96, 300–37; *Cart. Mon. Ram.* i, pp.423–8; *Select Pleas*, pp.xii–xiii, 6–9.
[3] *Stratton Ct. Rolls*, p.21.
[4] P.R.O. SC6/866/1; B.L. Egerton MS. 3308, f.7.
[5] F.G. Emmison, *Guide to Essex Record Office* (2nd edn, Chelmsford, 1969), pp.112, 127, 144.

seen at Ramsey Abbey, is very uncommon. Our usual record of a medieval manorial court is a roll of which there is no draft or duplicate and which often was demonstrably written, entry by entry, while the court was actually in progress, not copied out afterwards from a draft. On the other hand there seems to be no consistency between one estate and another in the way the rolls of individual courts were arranged. Sometimes the courts for each manor would be recorded one after the other on a single roll, as the steward made his way round the estate; we find this in the early court rolls from the Bec Abbey estates and, later, in Durham Cathedral Priory's rolls. Or successive courts on a particular manor might be entered on a single roll or file; in the late thirteenth century this was probably the more usual practice and it was adopted on the Bec Abbey estates in the early fourteenth century. But often the rolls were less systematically kept and we find individual pieces of parchment with just one or two courts entered on them, either from a single manor or from successive manors on a single circuit. Medieval manorial court rolls in fact varied a good deal in size and shape; to take two extreme examples, both from Bedfordshire, nearly all the courts for the Loring family's manor of Chalgrave from 1278 to 1313 are entered on a single roll 20 feet long, new membranes being added as court followed court, while another early-fourteenth-century court roll, from Eggington, measures less than 5 inches square.[6] On a few estates books were used instead of rolls for the formal record of the court; at Durham the bishopric, manor courts (*halmotes*, as often elsewhere) were recorded in volumes, while on the cathedral priory estates halmote books were used from 1400 to record the courts' land transactions, all other business still being entered on rolls. Increasingly in the fifteenth century we find that the formal record was not drawn up in the court itself but was a fair copy written afterwards from a draft or notes. Already in the 1420s at Canterbury Cathedral Priory the court rolls were compiled at the end of each year from the much fuller – and much untidier – notes made in the courts; the drafts were on paper, the fair copies on parchment, a distinction that we often find in the post-medieval records of manorial courts. Notes by the steward or his clerk that very occasionally survive from late-medieval manorial courts may have served either as a draft record or as memoranda.[7]

The formal record of its proceedings would not be the only written document that the medieval manorial court produced: it is just that others have seldom survived. Lists of estreats must have been drawn up after practically every session of a court, yet, as we have seen (above, p.39), we have few medieval examples. The note of cases to be heard at a forthcoming court that we have from Cuxham (Oxfordshire) in 1310 may also be simply the rare survivor of a common type of document, as also the list of those admitted to frankpledge that we have from Wreyland (Devon) in 1434.[8] In the course of time, developments in the courts and their procedures produced some new sorts of record. The copy of court roll is the most notable example. This was not a copy of an entire manorial court roll, but a copied extract recording the admission of a tenant into land or other property held by the local customary tenure of the manor; this would serve

---

[6] *Court Roll of Chalgrave Manor 1278–1313*, ed. Marian K. Dale, Bedfordshire Historical Record Soc. xxviii (1950), p.vii; Bedford County Record Office, X 310.

[7] e.g. muniments of Winchester College, 16743a (late 14th century); Worcester County Record Office, 009: 1 BA 2636/18 43762–43765 (1528–39).

[8] *Cuxham Man. Recs.* pp.632–3; *Wreyland Docs.* pp.71–2 (cf. *Ct. Baron*, p.69).

not as a title deed, but as useful evidence of when he entered his holding and on what terms. Copies of court roll are mentioned on the St. Albans Abbey estates in 1311 and on the manor of Wakefield (Yorkshire) in 1315,[9] but they probably spread rather slowly and it is uncommon to find actual copies earlier than the sixteenth century. The development of the copy of court roll reflects the increasing use of written records in manorial administration and the growing formality of procedure in the manorial court.

The official who held the manorial court was generally called the steward (*senescallus*) and his name is often given in the heading of the court roll. In the thirteenth and fourteenth centuries the roll would normally be written by a clerk who accompanied him to the court. Where we find that the hand in a series of court rolls changes at the point where a new steward takes over this merely implies that the clerk was appointed (and paid) by the steward, not by the lord of the manor; thus a new steward would probably mean a new clerk. But in the later middle ages, when only a draft, not the finished court roll, was written in the court, the steward seems usually to have written this draft himself and to have dispensed with a clerk. In the Paston letters we are told in 1470 how the rival claimant to a manor sat by the steward in the court and 'blotted his book with his finger as he wrote'.[10] Significantly, a printed treatise of 1510 on how to hold a manorial court says that, at the start, 'The steward who holds the court shall write the title in this way on paper . . .'[11] – paper suggests a draft, not the definitive record.

Various aids were available for those who held manorial courts or who wrote or used their records. Glossaries of the terms used, particularly archaic ones, occur in memorandum books and cartularies, and so too do sets of the questions that the steward was expected to put to the court at each meeting. The steward also had treatises to help him; most are simple guides to procedure, rather like those written for the auditors of manorial accounts, but two are very much fuller, giving in dialogue that is both picturesque and dramatic a complete narrative of what might occur at a meeting of the court – we have nothing comparable for the manorial audit. The earliest treatises for stewards date from the late thirteenth century, the first of a long series, for guides to keeping manorial courts continued to be produced down to the nineteenth century. The treatise of 1510 was the first to be printed; it was an anonymous work which lies entirely in the medieval tradition, but which went through some twenty editions down to 1650. Besides the treatises for stewards we find also specimen texts, some with added instructions, for the clerks who drew up the court rolls; again, the earliest date from the late thirteenth century.

Types of court
The private or seignorial courts for which we have most (but still not much) evidence from the twelfth century are the honour courts that a magnate would hold for an entire estate, or honour; a very large estate might comprise several honours with a separate court for each. Those who were required to attend the court – in medieval phraseology those who owed suit there, the suitors (*sectatores*)

<hr>

[9] Levett, *Studies*, p.139; *Court Rolls of the Manor of Wakefield*, ed. W.P. Baildon and others, Yorkshire Archaeological Soc. (5v., 1901–45), iii, p.149.
[10] *The Paston Letters*, ed. N. Davis (Oxford, 3v., 1971–), i, p.552.
[11] *Mod. Ten. Cur.* pp.1, 34.

– would be some or all of the free tenants of the honour. We know of these courts in the twelfth century only through occasional chance references in charters and chronicles and we know next to nothing of their business or how they conducted it. By the mid thirteenth century, when we start to have written rolls of their proceedings, it is clear that these honour courts were in decay – probably many had stopped being held. We have records from 1258 of Ramsey Abbey's honour court, which met at Broughton (Huntingdonshire), but as F.W. Maitland remarks 'The Abbot seems to have been at great and often fruitless pains to get suitors to attend, but when the court met it had next to no business to do', so that the record of its three-weekly meetings tells us little more than the names of defaulters and the various penalties and constraints placed upon them.[12] Even so, some such courts continued long in existence. The last surviving roll of Durham Cathedral Priory's court for its free tenants dates from 1425, by which time it was a record mostly of penalties for non-attendance, but the court was still nominally in existence in the 1460s, when its profits were said to be a consistent 6s. 0d. a year.[13] These honour courts were not manorial courts – they belonged to a higher level of seignorial administration – but they sometimes took over functions that more often belonged to manorial courts. Thus even the all but vestigial free tenants' court of Durham Cathedral Priory in 1400 summoned all the brewers from one manor to answer for offences against the assize of ale – business that one would expect to be done in a manorial court, at a view of frankpledge.[14]

The basis of the manorial court was the right of every landlord to hold a court for his local tenants, free and villein.[15] We have seen that by the fifteenth century the existence of such a court was being taken to define a property as a manor (above, p.2). This was the court that was known by the fifteenth century as a court baron.[16] Its rights of jurisdiction were limited, but were important within the local community. The law it administered was not imposed on it from outside but consisted of the customs of the particular manor, customs which varied from place to place and also, more than was commonly admitted, from one generation to another on a single manor. Within this framework it regulated the tenure of the villein or customary tenants, those who held their lands by the customs of the manor and who had only this court to turn to in any dispute or complaint about their tenure: a royal court of common law would refuse to hear them, on the grounds that they lay solely within the jurisdiction of their manorial lord. Everything to do with their lands and tenures would be dealt with there. Admission to a customary holding with imposition of an entry fine would be by formal ceremony in the court, so would its voluntary surrender; a tenant's death would be reported there with the heriot thereupon due (commonly the dead man's best beast) and his heir, defined by local custom, would be admitted there to succeed him. The terms and obligations of his tenure would be settled by the court, it was there that any failure to render due services would be dealt with, and

---

[12] *Select Pleas*, pp.50, 52–68.

[13] D. & C. Durham, Loc. iv, 237 and Bursars' Accounts 1466–7 onwards.

[14] D.& C. Durham, Halmote Court Rolls, autumn 1400 (Wolviston).

[15] Arguably, in the early 13th century, only with the consent of the manorial lord's overlord if the manor was not held directly of the Crown; thus Gilbert de Gant specifically gave Bridlington Priory (Yorks.) the right to hold a court for its tenants in Edenham (Lincs.) (B.L. Add. MS. 40008, f. 291).

[16] e.g. 'quedam Curia Baronis' in an inquisition of 1443 (B.L. Egerton MS. 3308, f.7); in the thirteenth century the phrase was applied to any seignorial court (thus *Ct. Baron*, pp.20, 62)

there that he would seek permission to sublet or exchange lands or to acquire
further land from other sources. It was there too that customary payments due
from the villein would be imposed: for permision to live away from the manor
(chevage: *capitagium*), to send his son to school or to enter holy orders, for his
daughter's marriage (merchet) or for an unmarried woman's unchastity (leyr-
wite). The manor's free tenants also had to attend the court, but it did not have
the same control of their lands and tenures – though fealty on entry, and
sometimes other procedures, might be performed there, and in the many sorts of
local tenure that developed in the fourteenth and fifteenth centuries the
distinction between customary and free, contractual tenure was often much
blurred, all being dealt with in the manorial court by more or less the same
procedures.

Free and customary tenants were at all times equally involved in the other
business of the court: oversight of the rural community and its lands, and the
settlement of disputes among its inhabitants (unless blood was shed, which was
breach of the king's peace). Where a manor comprised an entire vill, and where
that vill had common fields, the court's work in regulating their use was
especially important: the times for throwing the fields open to common grazing,
the rights of gleaning, trespass in the corn by men or livestock, encroachment
beyond the fixed boundaries, all fell within the court's purview. Sometimes
specific rules, by-laws (*bileges*), were formulated to record agreed custom on
particular points – agrarian or tenurial or sometimes on the more general aspects
of community life that the court dealt with: harbouring of strangers, movement
at night, and so on. Finally, it was in the manorial court that the lord's officials
would be elected by the court or nominated by the lord – it is not always clear
which, for custom varied from manor to manor. These officials would include the
reeve (if the manor was being run in demesne and not leased out) and one
variously known as the hayward, beadle or reap-reeve (*haiwardus, bedellus,
messor*) whose job was to guard the corn in the field and to present to the court
those who trespassed or did other damage to it.

Grafted on to this basic manorial court might be other wider rights of
jurisdiction which belonged to the Crown but which had been given to a local
manorial lord. The most common was the exercise within the manor of a bundle
of judicial rights which came to be known as the court leet. This name was in use
by the late fourteenth century,[17] but in the middle ages they were usually called
by the name of just one of these rights, the view of frankpledge (*visus franciplegii*),
it being understood that this included the others as well. View of frankpledge
itself was a relic of the system of mutual sureties or borhs, the frankpledge
system, that dated from long before the Norman Conquest: all males over twelve
were placed in groups of about ten whose members were held responsible for
each other's lawful behaviour. By the late thirteenth century nothing was left of
the system except the formality of seeing that all men belonged, at least in theory,
to one of these so-called tithing groups (*decenne*); this was done by the view of
frankpledge, which enquired – in the oddly back-to-front contemporary phrase –
whether all the tithing groups were full, a procedure which brought the court
some small takings from those who were not in tithing groups but which now

---

[17] As on a court roll from Fawley (Bucks.) in 1378 that is headed 'Curia cum Let" (B.L. Add.
Roll 27029).

contributed little to local law and order. The other rights that went with view of frankpledge were less notional. They still included in the fourteenth century the right to maintain a gallows and to hang any thief caught red-handed within the manor,[18] as well as the right to try minor breaches of the king's peace involving wounding; the court's criminal jurisdiction was steadily eroded, however, and in 1461 it lost its right even to present serious, indictable offences to the royal courts.[19] They also included maintaining the assizes of bread and ale, that is ensuring that what was sold by bakers or brewers within the manor met required standards of quality and quantity. This odd mixture of rights also involved choosing officials in the court; the most usual are the ale-tasters (*tastatores cervisie*) and the head of each tithing group – the chief pledge, tithingman or headborough (i.e. head borh: *capitalis plegius, decennarius*). Where this jurisdiction had not been given to the manorial lord it would be exercised for the Crown by the sheriff in the local hundred court. View of frankpledge was one of the franchises that were called in question by the *Quo Warranto* enquiries of the 1270s, but the statute of *Quo Warranto* in 1290, which recognised long use as a sufficient title, left the lords of many manors in possession of view of frankpledge and the other rights that went with it. Sometimes not just view of frankpledge within the manor but the entire hundred court would belong to some specially privileged manorial lord – the hundred courts of west Suffolk held by the abbey of Bury St Edmunds are an outstanding example. The hundred would be regarded as appurtenant to a particular manor and the manorial court would serve as the hundred court as well.

The distinction between court baron and court leet is clear to the historian and it was clear too, under whatever names, to medieval lawyers and Crown officials. It was less clear at the local level, however, and records of manorial courts that had view of frankpledge sometimes seem to confuse the two types of jurisdiction. Often the manorial court met more frequently than was necessary for the court-leet business, which required only two sessions a year;[20] these sessions may or may not be identified in the heading of the court roll as 'Court with view of frankpledge' (*Curia cum visu franciplegii*) or more vaguely by some such phrase as 'Great court' (*Magna curia*). In the thirteenth and fourteenth centuries the business at these sessions was often jumbled together, so that the roll does not show whether a particular item derives from one jurisdiction or the other.

More often than not a single manorial court, with or without view of frankpledge, was held for a single manor. But there were more complicated structures of courts. This might reflect complications in the manorial structure. In the early thirteenth century the bishop of Winchester's large and complex manor of Taunton (Somerset) had two simple manorial courts at Corfe and Holway to deal with court-baron business for the manor, a hundred court which administered view of frankpledge not only for the bishop's manor but also for the rest of the hundred, and possibly a separate court for the borough of Taunton

---

[18] It has been suggested that this right was lost in the 13th century (thus Hearnshaw, *Leet Jur.* pp.101–2), but one late-13th-century treatise shows us the steward apparently sentencing a thief to death on conviction (*Ct. Baron*, pp.62–4) and Merton College, Oxford, tried and hanged a horse-thief on its manor of Holywell, Oxford, in 1337 (J.E.T. Rogers, *A History of Agriculture and Prices in England* (Oxford, 7v., 1866–1902), ii, p.666).

[19] By the act of 1 Edward IV, c.2.

[20] The 1217 and 1225 (and subsequent) reissues of Magna Carta laid down that the sheriff in the hundred court should hold a view of frankpledge only twice a year, after Easter and after Michaelmas.

itself.[21] On the other hand in the fifteenth century the bishop of Lincoln probably had a single court for his complex of properties centred on Banbury (Oxfordshire), combining in it the functions of hundred court and of manorial court for both the town and the rural manors; however, there was a special court held for Banbury's annual fair (known, as elsewhere, as a court of pie powder: *curia pedis pulveris*) and by 1476 a separate portmoot was being held for the town.[22] Even where the manorial structure was simpler complications might occur. Crowland Abbey had three separate manors to the north-east of Cambridge, but had a single manorial court for all three; on many of its thirteenth- and fourteenth-century court rolls a marginal letter shows which manor each entry belongs to (*c* for Cottenham, *d* for Dry Drayton, *h* for *Hokington*', i.e. Oakington).[23] We must also remember that a single property would lie within more than one manor at different levels of feudal tenure. Merton College had a court for its manor of Cuxham (Oxfordshire), a property which it held of the honour of Wallingford, but the view of frankpledge remained in the hands of the overlord; this right was administered through the neighbouring manor of Chalgrove, so it is on the court rolls of Chalgrove that we find Cuxham's view of frankpledge.[24] In using manorial court rolls we must be prepared for some variety in the structure of local courts and rights of jurisdiction.

Court procedure and terminology

Despite these differences in structure and jurisdiction, despite some variation from region to region and from manor to manor, much of the procedure and terminology of manorial courts was common to all. We see this in the frequency with which courts were held. In principle a lord could require a free tenant to attend his court every three weeks and some courts of every kind were in fact held as often as this: Ramsey Abbey's honour court at Broughton in the mid thirteenth century, for instance, or the bishop of Lincoln's portmoot at Banbury and the court of the royal manor of Bromsgrove (Worcestershire) in the late fifteenth. Earl Warenne's manor court at Wakefield sometimes met even more often. Suitors, however, were not necessarily required to attend every meeting: Durham Cathedral Priory's court for its free tenants met every three weeks, but some tenants had to attend only five times a year, some only three times. Many courts met much less often than this. Adam de Stratton's court at Sevenhampton (Wiltshire) in the 1270s and 1280s met about eight times a year, the prior of Merton's court at Tooting Bec (Surrey) in the early fifteenth century twice a year, the Dynham family's court at Wreyland (Devon) in the 1480s and 1490s from one to three times. Some courts were held both irregularly and infrequently, and years might elapse between meetings, urgent business such as admission to holdings being done privately by the lord or his officials. This irregularity can make it difficult to tell how far a surviving series of court rolls is complete; sometimes, however, manorial accounts, in entering the profits from the court, will give the dates on which it was held, and sometimes we can use entries of essoins to tell whether court rolls are missing.

Essoins (*essonie*) are excuses, in effect apologies for absence. They are entered

---

[21] *Winch. Pipe Roll 1210–11*, pp.164–7.
[22] *V.C.H. Oxon.* x, p.72.
[23] Page, *Crowland*, pp.331–2, 368–70, etc.
[24] *Cuxham Man. Recs.* p. 72.

on the court roll with the names of those nominated by the absent suitors to stand proxy for them. A suitor was generally allowed an essoin on up to three consecutive occasions; the court-roll entry may thus say that it is the first, second or third time, and this is how we can sometimes tell whether any rolls are missing from the surviving series.[25] The entry of essoin will say too whether the absentee had been summoned for a particular case or simply by virtue of his regular obligation to attend for common suit (de communi).

Much of the business of the court came to it by presentments, that is reports or accusations made in answer to specific questions put by the steward. The court rolls preserve the answers, the presentments, but not the questions asked, though we have specimen sets of questions in contemporary notes and treatises.[26] Some presentments were made by officials; thus the hayward commonly presented the names of those he had caught trespassing in the corn. But others were made by the manorial jury (juratores), a group of usually about a dozen local tenants, free or villein; where a single court met for more than one manor, or where a single manor included several vills, there might be more than one jury, and sometimes a separate jury would be chosen for court-leet business. The manorial jury seems to have emerged in the late thirteenth and early fourteenth centuries and the presentment procedure may have originated then. Besides making presentments in answer to the steward's questions the jury would be referred to for statements of manorial custom as well as for decisions in cases brought by one villager against another: the person accused would, in the record's phrase, place himself on the country (ponit se super patriam) and the jury would then declare the truth of the matter one way or the other. Here the manorial jury seems to have taken over functions that had formerly belonged to the entire body of suitors, and the way its decisions are said to be made by 'the homage' or 'the whole court' (homagium, tota curia) preserves a memory of this. Alternatively the party to a plea might be allowed to prove his case by compurgation, waging his law (vadiat legem, ponit se ad legem), producing in court say three or six supporters as required (ad terciam manum, ad sextam manum) to swear to the truth of his story.

Apart from inflicting penalties the manorial court had two ways of constraining people to attend its meetings or to comply with its orders. One was distraint, seizure of property, to be returned only when the court's demand had been met – a common device in medieval legal procedures in general, but at the humble level of the manorial court effectively confined to seizure of chattels and often referred to not as distraint but as attachment.[27] The hayward would, for instance, take from any stranger found trespassing on the corn some piece of personal property which could be recovered only by attending the court and accepting its penalty. Or the court might order an official to distrain or attach (distringere, attachiare: the two words are used indifferently) someone who allegedly owed suit to the court but who consistently failed to attend. The other way the court would try to enforce compliance was by the personal pledge or surety: one or more tenants of the manor, generally of fairly high standing in the community, would make

---

[25] e.g. entries of the first and third essoins of John de Riston' show that one, and only one, court was held at Oakington between the meetings of 14 December 1290 and 14 May 1291 (Page, Crowland, pp.331, 333).

[26] These sets of 'articles' for the view of frankpledge are discussed, and fourteenth-century examples printed, by Hearnshaw, Leet Jur. pp.24–5, 30–2, 43–64, 373–5.

[27] This attachment of chattels is to be distinguished from the more usual medieval use of the word, attachment of the person or arrest.

themselves responsible for what was required (and would incur penalties in case of failure). Someone distrained to attend the court, for instance, might find a manorial tenant to be his pledge (*plegius*, with verb *plegiare*), to stand surety for him, on which the property distrained would be restored to him. But pledges appear most often in manorial court rolls as sureties for penal or other payments levied by the court; even if the payment was due from a tenant of high standing one or two others would still be named as his pledges – indeed, where two or more tenants were both amerced for a particular offence they might be pledges to each other (*plegii alter alterius*). Just why one man would agree to stand pledge to another in this way is not wholly clear, though recent studies have analysed the pattern of personal pledging in manorial court rolls so as to establish the patterns of personal relationships within the medieval village; it seems as if sometimes, at least, the pledge was paid for his services by the person pledged, so that the system may have brought some profit to those whom the court would accept as pledges.[28] Pledging seems generally to have disappeared from manorial courts in the late fourteenth or early fifteenth century.

A payment imposed by a manorial court might be called a fine (*finis*). This was not a penal payment; in origin and in the royal courts it was payment made, by agreement, to conclude a case. In the manorial court the word was applied to various sorts of agreed payments: an entry fine on admission to a customary tenement, for instance, or payment for permission to bring a case before the court. Penal payments were of two sorts. If the court made an order, either in an individual case or of general application, it would often define the penalty (*pena*), usually a substantial sum, due from the offender who failed to comply; if this penalty were actually imposed it would again be called *pena*. But the more usual payment was the far smaller amercement (*amerciamentum*, but in court rolls usually *misericordia*); the offence was held to have placed the offender at the lord's mercy, and the amercement extricated him from this position. If the offence was admitted the offender might be said to have placed himself at mercy (*ponit se in misericordia;* note the risk of confusion with *ponit se super patriam* or *ponit se ad legem*, for all three may be abbreviated to *ponit se* alone). The amounts of the amercements were fixed not by the steward but by affeerors (*afferatores*). Usually there were two, chosen from among the better placed manorial tenants, free or unfree; the treatise of 1510 tells us that this was done at the end of the court's other business.[29]

Some payments, especially in views of frankpledge, were made not because an offence had been committed but by way of compounding for penalties that might be imposed if it were ever presented. We see this in the enquiries into the tithing groups themselves. Instead of presenting individuals who had to be placed in a tithing group, some manors, or particular vills or hamlets within a manor, would pay an agreed regular sum which was understood to absolve them from all further obligation on this score; this was known as certainty money (*certum*), later as cert money or cert. Similarly with the assize of ale: those who brewed for sale would make a regular annual payment not for actual breaches of the assize but in effect for licence to brew without risk of presentment for any breach that might occur.

Administering the customary tenure of lands made up much of the business of

---

[28] e.g. M. Pimsler, 'Solidarity in the Medieval Village? The Evidence of Personal Pledging at Elton, Huntingdonshire', *Journal of British Studies*, xvii (1977–8), pp.1–11.
[29] *Mod. Ten. Cur.* p.25.

most manorial courts: accepting the surrender of holdings, admitting new tenants and so on. This is recorded in a vocabulary that is technical but mostly quite straightforward. Two phrases, however, call for explanation. In some court rolls a customary tenant is said to be admitted 'by the rod' (*per virgam*), a reference to the stick carried by the steward which would be used in a ceremony of admission to a holding (see below, pp.61–2, 63); this sort of custom varied from manor to manor, and on some admission is said to be by a straw. The only way a customary tenant could relinquish a holding was to surrender it to the manorial lord, who would then admit a new tenant; but the lord would commonly accept a surrender in favour of some specified prospective tenant with whom the retiring tenant had come to some agreement (whether for family reasons or against payment), and in this case the holding was said to be surrendered 'for the use' (*ad opus*) of the person concerned, who would then at once be admitted.

The court roll: form and contents

The manorial court roll of the mid or late thirteenth century seems a formless document when we think of the standardised layout and headings of contemporary manorial accounts and extents. It starts with a heading giving the name of the manor and the date of the court. The first entries that follow are generally the essoins. In the left-hand margin of the roll, opposite the relevant entries, are written the amounts of amercements or other payments due and brief (usually one-word) notes of action ordered or taken by the court: 'enquiry', 'to be attached' (*inquisitio, attachietur*), and so on. It can sometimes be shown that these notes in the margin were written after the rest of the roll, at the end of the court's business, when the affeerors did their work of assessing the amercements. Beyond this the court roll has no formal structure (see Plate 7). The roll (or the draft, if a fair copy was made afterwards) will normally have been written entry by entry as business proceeded in the court itself; how this business was ordered is seldom clear and is certainly not made explicit by formal divisions or subheadings on the roll. In the course of the fourteenth and fifteenth centuries the court roll became longer and more formalised and, on many manors, more methodically arranged. This process can be seen in any substantial series of medieval court rolls, but it has never been examined in detail. All we can do here is to note some of its more usual features, with, as some guide to their chronology, the dates when they first appear on four published series of court rolls (Figure 4).

One standard practice that developed was to remove the name of the manor from the heading of the roll, placing it instead in the margin to the left. The heading itself, however, came to be expanded by naming the lord of the manor and also the steward who held the court. Elsewhere in the roll too there was an increasing tendency to give the names of those with particular responsibilities; the manorial jury would be listed and after the final entry of the court's business the affeerors would be named. The total amount of the various payments imposed by the court also came to be entered at the end of the roll, often with a note of the steward's expenses in cash and in provisions so that the net profit of the court could be worked out. Another development was that the presentments of a single official – the hayward's for trespass in the corn, for instance – would be identified as such and brought together in a single paragraph. In cases like this, where a single entry listed people who were all amerced or owed some other payment, the amount due from each would be written above the individual

Manor[a]	Wakefield (Yorks.)	Cuxham (Oxon.)	Elton (Hunts.)	Oakington (Cambs.)
Lord	Earls Warenne	Merton College, Oxford	Ramsey Abbey	Crowland Abbey
Period covered	1274–1331	1276–1359	1279–1350	1290–1430
Name of manor in left margin	–	1323	1279	1319
Lord of manor named in heading	–	1343	–	1391
Steward named in heading	1275	1343	1294	1318
Manorial juries named	1275	–	1279	1327
Affeerors named	1326	1329	1350	1403
Entry of total payments imposed	1274	1298	1279	1318
Entry of steward's expenses	–	1358	–	1318
Official's presentments listed in single paragraph	1307[b]	1343[b]	1294	1357
Individuals' payments entered above names, total in margin	1331	1303	1350[c]	1319

A dash means that the innovation does not appear in the published series.

a For the published editions see pp.12n, 53–4
b Official making the presentments not identified
c Many earlier Elton court rolls are fair copies and on the drafts the practice may have occurred long before.

Figure 4. Dates of innovations in manorial court rolls from four published series

names, with a single total in the margin. We find another move towards greater orderliness in the occasional clear separation of the view of frankpledge from the rest of the court business and, where the court covered more than one manor or vill, a tendency for the entries for each place to be brought together on the roll. Thus at Oakington, where the court also served the neighbouring manors of Cottenham and Dry Drayton, successive rolls of courts with view of frankpledge from 1290 to 1339 show the court-leet business being gradually defined and brought together, manor by manor, the rest of the business following at the end for all three manors indiscriminately.

Many of these moves towards greater orderliness and formality on the court roll cannot be precisely dated or even defined. The entries of admission to customary holdings, for instance, become gradually longer and more formal, while presentments of misdemeanours of one sort or another are likely to be entered in set phrases without the circumstantial detail of some earlier court rolls – greater legal precision may here be the historian's loss. If successive court rolls get longer in the course of the fourteenth century they are not necessarily more informative. But sometimes they are. Thus increased reliance on the written record meant that it became more common to enter by-laws, specific statements of manorial custom, on the roll, at first on individual points as they arose, but by the mid fourteenth century in the form of whole codes of local customs or ordinances.

Changes in the court roll may also reflect changes in the business done in the manorial court. We even see a change in the function of the court and of its chairman, the steward: in the mid thirteenth century he might be primarily an estate manager, who held the manorial court as only one of many duties in supervising the estate's agriculture and other business, whereas by the early fourteenth century he was nearly everywhere employed solely to hold the courts and perhaps to serve on the lord's council. This change underlies the court rolls' tendency to greater precision and formality but can also appear in their contents: only very early court rolls include entries concerning the agricultural management of the manor, such as the note of implements given to the reeve at Steeple Ashton (Wiltshire) in 1262 or the estimate of unthreshed corn at Newton and Melbourn (Cambridgeshire) in 1282[30] Many later changes in the detailed contents of court rolls arise through changes in rural society itself. We find in the course of the fourteenth century, for instance, that fewer people make payments for breaches of assize of ale (as we have seen, effectively simply for licence to brew for sale) but that each of them has brewed more often – a result of the growth of specialised brewers and the emergence of the village alehouse. Again we see changes following the loss of population in the mid fourteenth century in increasing presentments of villeins who have left the manor, and of tenants who have failed to keep their buildings in repair: because land was easily available two or more former holdings would now be held by a single tenant who would have no use for the extra houses and other buildings. Often entries of admission to holdings become longer on the roll because the terms and conditions of tenure are set out in full – reflecting the multiplicity of local tenures that developed in the late fourteenth and fifteenth centuries on terms that varied not just from one manor to another but from one tenant to the next. All this is a measure of the value of manorial court rolls as evidence for the changes occurring in the countryside of late-medieval England.

Select texts

Select Pleas, pp.6–47. Courts of the manors of Bec Abbey, 1246–96. Proceedings of some courts in full, from others only select entries (omissions are indicated). Latin text with translation.

Select Pleas, pp.52–85. Honour court of Ramsey Abbey at Broughton (Hunts.), 1258, 1293–5. Proceedings in 1258 in full, but some omissions (indicated) from the rest. Latin text with translation.

Court Rolls of the Manor of Wakefield, ed. W.P. Baildon, S. Lister and J.W. Walker, Yorkshire Archaeological Soc. Record Ser. (5v., 1901–45); ed. Helen M. Jewell and Sue S. Walker, Yorkshire Archaeological Soc. Wakefield Court Rolls Ser. ii, iii (1981–3). Manorial court with view of frankpledge, 1274–1333, 1348–50. English translation, with (in the first volume, pp.1–156) Latin text of the rolls for 1274–5.

Stratton Ct. Rolls, pp.25–110. Manorial court of Sevenhampton, with view of frankpledge, 1275–88. Latin text.

The Rolls of Highworth Hundred 1275–1287, ed. Brenda A. Farr, Wiltshire Record Soc. xxi, xxii (1966–8). Private hundred court. Latin text.

---

[30] *Select Pleas*, p.183n; Cambridge University Library, D. & C. Ely.

Cuxham Man. Recs. pp.607–709. Manorial court without view of frankpledge, 1279–1358. Latin text.

Page, *Crowland*, pp.331–448. Manorial court of Oakington, with Cottenham and Dry Drayton (Cambs.), with view of frankpledge, 1290–1430. Latin text.

Court Rolls of Tooting Beck Manor, ed. G.L. Gomme (London County Council, 1909). Manorial court of Tooting Bec, with Streatham (Surrey), with view of frankpledge, 1394–1422. Latin text with translation.

Wreyland Docs. pp.1–70. Manorial court of Wreyland (Devon), with view of frankpledge, 1437–41, 1477–1501. Latin text with translation.

The Court Rolls of the Manor of Bromsgrove and King's Norton 1494–1504, ed. A.F.C. Baber. Manorial court with view of frankpledge. Analytical calendar in English, with the full Latin text of the roll for 1494–5.

See also the select texts for chapter 5 (below, p.67) for further fifteenth- and sixteenth-century court rolls.

Further reading

More has been written on court rolls than on other medieval manorial records, and it is surprising that we have not more precise information on development of their form and contents. The introduction to *Select Pleas* is of basic importance; the introduction to *Stratton Ct. Rolls* provides a valuable discussion of the various court procedures and court-roll entries; the introduction to *Cuxham Man. Recs.* pp.78–83, offers slightly more detail than is given here on the composition of the court roll. None of these looks later than the mid fourteenth century. An unpublished thesis by J.S. Beckerman, 'Customary Law in English Manorial Courts in the Thirteenth and Fourteenth Centuries' (London University Ph.D. thesis, 1972), is an important study of the developments in forms and procedures during this period. The frankpledge system to about 1300 is described by W.A Morris, *The Frankpledge System* (New York, 1910); D.A. Crowley, 'The Later History of Frankpledge', *Bulletin of the Institute of Historical Research*, xlviii (1975), pp.1–15, discusses its later decline from the records of five Essex villages. The history and distribution of manors with hundred courts attached are discussed by Helen M. Cam, *Liberties and Communities in Medieval England* (Cambridge, 1944), pp.64–90. Z. Razi, 'The Toronto School's Reconstitution of Medieval Peasant Society: a Critical View', *Past and Present*, lxxxv (1979), pp.141–57, draws attention to some of the risks in using court-roll evidence for the individuals and the social structure of the medieval village. Four treatises of the thirteenth and early fourteenth centuries are published in *Ct. Baron* and the printed treatise of 1510 is reprinted in *Mod. Ten. Cur.*

CHAPTER V

MANORIAL RECORDS AFTER 1540

The post-medieval manorial court

We have seen that by the fifteenth century a new definition of the manor was emerging: a property was a manor only if its owner held a court for his tenants – a court baron, that is, with or without court leet. This was the generally accepted meaning of the word from the sixteenth century onwards as well as its technical legal meaning. A large landed estate might still include several or many manors. But it would also include properties with tenants for whom the owner held no court, properties which thus were not manors and never could become manors, for it was held that no new court baron or manor could be created (though arguably an existing manor might be enlarged). Indeed it came to be said that a lawful manor must have existed time out of mind,[1] that is from the limit of legal memory in 1189, though in fact many manors would not have stood up to this historical test: new manors and manorial courts were being set up in the fifteenth century. An estate, then, would include some units that formed manors and others that did not, and for most day-to-day purposes the same administrative methods would be applied to both sorts of property and the same sorts of record created. Where a property formed a manor it would often be called a manor in these records; there might be a map of the manor, or a manorial rent-roll, or an inventory of the manor's standing timber. But these were normal records for the running of any landed estate; the only records peculiar to manors as such were the records generated by the manorial court. It is only with manorial records in this restricted, technical sense that we are concerned.

Even so, the sheer quantity of these records that survive from the mid sixteenth century onwards is far greater than that of the wider range of manorial records from earlier periods. By and large they have had better chances of survival than other records of landed estates. Their formality, the legal significance attaching to them, their appeal to antiquarian-minded estate owners and lawyers who would think them worthier of preservation than other more mundane (though often more informative) records, and finally the protection offered since 1926 by the Manorial Documents Rules (above, p.11) have all contributed to this. In view of the bulk of these later records it may seem unreasonable to have devoted so much more space to the records of medieval manorial administration. This, however, merely reflects the greater technical difficulties of these earlier records and also their historical importance. They are by far our most informative source of evidence not only on the organisation of landed estates in medieval England but on the whole structure of rural economy and society. For the local historian, where there are manorial records they will be the fullest, often the only detailed, records of the medieval village community. The records of post-medieval manorial courts are simply not comparable. They are at best only one source among many for the history of the English countryside in the period and even for the topics they tell us most about, such as local tenures or common rights, they seldom give a comprehensive picture. At the same time

---

[1] Coke, *Copy-Holder*, pp.52–3, 56–7; *A Manor and Court Baron*, ed. N.J. Hone, Manorial Soc. iii (1909), p.13.

they should not be underestimated. Even where other sources exist they may still give the local historian invaluable information on the tenants, the buildings and the topography of the manor. And for the early part of the period we find some manorial courts involved in aspects of local government and in maintaining law and order in the community.

There was no marked change in the function of the court baron in the sixteenth century, and developments in the post-medieval manorial court mostly continued existing trends. As before, we find the court regulating agriculture, in manors where tenants held rights in common, by individual orders or sets of by-laws which often become longer and more detailed than in the middle ages. Here, agricultural change might bring new complexities, as at Great Tew (Oxfordshire) in 1761, where the court, taking turnips, clover and sown grass into account, had to work out far more elaborate cropping sequences than the medieval winter corn, spring corn, fallow.[2] Other changes also affected the court's detailed business; a few miles away, at Deddington (Oxfordshire) in 1914 the manorial court amerced the Post Office 1s. for each of ten telegraph poles that it had put up.[3] However, the court's right to hear cases between individuals involving sums of up to 40s. was quite commonly exercised throughout the sixteenth century as it had been before 1540. And as before, the court administered customary tenure on the manor, and any change of tenant could be made only by surrender and admission in the court. Here, sixteenth-century developments, while not affecting the court baron's function, were significant for its status and, as we shall see, for its procedures: customary tenants who held copies of court roll could now bring cases touching their holdings to the royal courts – to the court of Chancery from Henry VII's reign, to other courts of equitable jurisdiction a little later, and to the common-law courts from the 1550s.[4] This made copyhold a recognised form of tenure which was still administered by the court baron and still dependent on local custom but which was now the subject of a growing body of case law and legal definition (and, it might be added, of historical myth) at the hands of the royal courts, their judges and lawyers.

Nor was there any radical change in the court leet. As we have already seen, it lost its right to present indictable offences in 1461. But the view of frankpledge, with its age-old enquiry into the tithing groups, already an archaism in the thirteenth century, continued in being on some manors – at Hanwell (Oxfordshire) certainty money was still being paid in 1904.[5] The assize of bread and ale continued, and so too did the duty of the court leet to choose the constable for the vill and to see that the king's peace was maintained there. Here, however, its function was overlapping with the newer, but well established, authority of the justices of the peace. Which was the more active, whether the constable made his presentments to the local justices or to the court leet, seems to have varied from place to place. Some statutes envisaged a kind of power-sharing with the justices of the peace and with the parish authorities, for they gave court leets powers to enquire into playing unlawful games (1541), upkeep of roads (1555), attendance at musters (1557), drunkenness (1607) and other matters.[6] Such statutes added

[2] Webb, *Manor*, i, pp.86–7.

[3] *V.C.H. Oxon.* xi, p.108.

[4] C.M. Gray, *Copyhold, Equity and the Common Law*, Harvard Historical Monographs, 53 (Cambridge, Mass., 1963), pp.23–92.

[5] *V.C.H. Oxon.* ix, p.4.

[6] A list of statutes between 1523 and 1624 that laid duties on the court leet is in Hearnshaw, *Leet Jur.* pp.122–30.

to the responsibilities of the court leet, and clearly by the late sixteenth century it was far from being regarded as defunct or archaic. In many towns, indeed, a court leet was an integral part of the structure of courts and other authorities which made up town government and which differed a good deal in detail from one town to another; it was here that the court leet was generally most resilient, often playing an active part in urban administration down to the Municipal Corporations Act of 1835. The court leet of the boroughs, the chartered towns, lies outside our scope, but it is interesting that in sixteenth-century Essex the amount of business done in a court leet seems to have reflected the economy of the manor: if it was purely agricultural the court leet would have little to do, but in places that were centres for traders and craftsmen it would be much more active.[7] This could be because its more practical responsibilities, whether ancient or newly laid on it by statute, tended to be particularly relevant to urban communities: standards of bread and ale, suppression of nuisances (in which certain trades, notably butchering and tanning, were frequent offenders), and the like.

In the sixteenth century, then, both court baron and court leet were reasonably thriving institutions. Some of their functions were outdated, but they still had a distinctive and useful role to play; they were still adapting to changing circumstances. After the late sixteenth century this was no longer so, and from then on the history of manorial courts is one of gradual but unrelenting decay. Their practical functions dropped away, and they ceased to meet or degenerated into mere jollifications or antiquarian play-acting. Everywhere the process was slow, and as it was governed mainly by local circumstances the chronology of the decline and disappearance of manorial courts differed a good deal from place to place. Three general developments contributed particularly to this decline, though how far and when again varied greatly from one manor to another. One was the gradual appropriation of responsibilities by two other authorities: the parish vestry or the township meeting, already dominant where manorial authority was divided or weakly exercised, and the justices of the peace, especially in the quarter sessions for the county, where a manorial court's claim to oversight of highways or bridges or other matters was apt to be overlooked unless vigorously asserted. The effect of this has been neatly demonstrated from the court rolls of Ightham (Kent): between 1586 and 1618 three-fifths of the business of the court was to do with public administration – the assizes of bread and ale, breaches of the peace, upkeep of bridges and fences, and so on – but after 1707 the court leet lapsed and thenceforward the court dealt only with matters of tenure and land transfers among the manorial tenants.[8] A second development which took business away from the manorial courts was the enclosure of common pastures and of arable in areas where there was common-field agriculture. This might be achieved by private agreement, as so often in the seventeenth century, or by private parliamentary act or, after 1836, under the General Enclosure Acts; however effected, enclosure at once did away with the need to regulate cropping and common-pasture practices, a widespread function of the manorial court. Finally, the decline of manorial courts was hastened by the decline of copyhold

---

[7] K.C. Newton and Marjorie K. McIntosh, 'Leet Jurisdiction in Essex Manor Courts during the Elizabethan Period', *Essex Archaeology and History*, xiii (1981), pp.3–14.

[8] E. Harrison, 'The Court Rolls and Other Records of the Manor of Ightham as a Contribution to Local History', *Archaeologia Cantiana*, xlviii (1936), p.185 and facing table.

tenure. Already in the seventeenth century it was held that copyhold, like the manor itself, could not be newly created. Land could be held in copyhold only if it had been so held for time immemorial, and any change of tenure – to leasehold or to freehold – extinguished the copyhold for ever: the land could never be held in copyhold again. It followed that the amount of copyhold land could only get smaller with the passage of time, and already in the sixteenth century it was being severely eroded as particular circumstances led both lord and tenant to find advantages in 'enfranchising' lands to be held freely or by lease. Even in 1799 Charles Watkins, author of a standard work on copyhold law, was arguing that this form of tenure had outlived its usefulness:

> The wisdom and expediency of a general law, to which all landed property should alike be subject, and the confusion and manifold evils which are inevitably attendant on a diversity of local customs, must be apparent to everyone . . . . As we have manifestly outlived the principles of copyhold-law, why should that law be continued? . . . Why must we be perpetually appealing to the fool's idol of precedent? Why be dissatisfied with common sense? May not what was just at one period, become, under other circumstances, unjust?[9]

But it was not until the 1922 Law of Property Act that the remnants of copyhold tenure were finally abolished. Where there was copyhold a manorial court was needed to administer it – indeed, the copyholders could insist that a court be held. Where copyhold tenure disappeared from a manor – often long before 1922 – the principal reason for holding the manorial court will normally have disappeared too.[10]

Even without copyhold tenure some manorial courts continued to meet after 1922. In 1977 the Administration of Justice Act ruled that manorial and some other ancient courts 'shall cease to have any jurisdiction to hear and determine legal proceedings', but that they could continue to do other business customary in the particular court; a schedule to the act listed thirty-two such courts, specifying what could be regarded as customary business for each.[11] A very few vestiges of manorial jurisdiction thus still survive today.

Sydney and Beatrice Webb, in their illuminating account of manorial courts between 1689 and 1835, had little good to say of them seeing them as inefficient, archaic survivals: 'It will be at once apparent that we are dealing with an institution that is nowhere in its prime, but in every instance falling into decay'.[12] We have seen how in the late eighteenth century Charles Watkins saw copyhold, the mainstay of the manorial court, as ripe for reform. But still by the nineteenth century possession of a manorial court might be seen as an enhancement of the dignity of a landed gentleman; Jane Austen writes without irony of the 'ancient manorial residence of the family, with all its rights of Court-Leet and Court-Baron'.[13] In the course of the nineteenth century surviving manorial courts, with their sometimes quaint customs, attracted the attention of local antiquaries and

---

[9] C. Watkins, *A Treatise on Copyholds* (London, 2v., 1797–9), ii, pp.203–4.
[10] H. Jenner-Fust, 'Hill, Gloucestershire', *Transactions of the Bristol and Gloucestershire Archaeological Society*, liii (1931), p.186, provides an example of a manorial court that did not outlive the end of copyhold on the manor; its last recorded meeting was in 1761. A list of courts leet that includes many surviving into the 19th century is given by Hearnshaw, *Leet Jur.* pp.248–321.
[11] 25 & 26 Elizabeth II, c. 38, section 23 and schedule 4.
[12] Webb, *Manor*, i, p.31.
[13] [Jane Austen], *Mansfield Park* (2nd edn, London, 3v., 1816), i, chapter 8.

those interested in folk-lore; thus the Devonshire Association set up a 'Committee to obtain information as to the peculiar tenures of lands and as to customs of manor courts, in Devonshire, exclusive of Dartmoor', which produced four reports between 1880 and 1884. Descriptions of the records of post-medieval manorial courts, often with substantial extracts, can be found in the published transactions of a number of local antiquarian societies. On the other hand, they have been largely overlooked by record-publishing societies, and hardly any have been systematically published. The Manorial Society, founded in 1906 with a membership drawn from lords and stewards of manors as well as interested historians and antiquaries, produced sixteen publications, the last in 1929, which included lists of manorial records and reprints of sixteenth- and seventeenth-century treatises but no editions of court rolls. Interestingly, the most substantial publication of these records was undertaken for a purely practical purpose: in 1866 one of the first acts of a private committee of local inhabitants and property-owners for the preservation of Wimbledon Common (Surrey) was to have printed a 600-page volume of extracts from the manorial court rolls relating to the rights of common in Wimbledon from the fifteenth century down to the present – a work of great value and interest even though it covers only one aspect of the court's business (see the select texts listed at the end of this chapter).

Types of court and procedure
One perceptive comment of Sydney and Beatrice Webb is that as procedures in manorial courts rested not on statutes or the common law but on local custom and the chairmanship of the lawyer who was steward, the manuals and treatises giving guidance on holding these courts were far more influential in governing and shaping their procedures than the similar works written for local justices and other authorities.[14] This was no doubt the case – but it should be added that it was no more than a continuation of a process that had begun at the end of the thirteenth century, when stewards began to be specialised legal officials rather than general estate managers. Certainly numerous manuals on holding manorial courts were published from the sixteenth century to the nineteenth,[15] but they form a single tradition with their medieval precursors. We have seen that the first printed manual, in 1510, was published in revised editions down to 1650, while we still find occasional echoes of its text even in the final (1819) edition of Giles Jacob's *Complete Court-Keeper*.[16] But the treatises of the seventeenth century onwards differed from the earlier ones in one important respect. Now that, since the 1550s, cases touching copyhold were being heard by the courts of common law, a whole body of legal precedents and definitions quickly built up, and the treatises thus came to include long sections of rulings over the tenure of copyhold land, a matter that had hitherto lain entirely within the discretion of the court baron, governed by local custom alone.

[14] Webb, *Manor*, i, pp.11–13.
[15] Lists are in Hearnshaw, *Leet Jur.* pp.32–42, and in Webb, *Manor*, i, pp.10n–11n (a few of the dates need amendment). Besides the printed manuals many circulated in manuscript; Webb, *Manor*, i, pp.35–6, describes one example, another (early 17th century) is University of London Library, Palaeography Room, Fuller Collection 4/43, and another (dated 1736) is printed by Canon Oldfield, 'Manor Courts', *Berks, Bucks and Oxon Archaeological Journal*, xix (1913), pp.75–80.
[16] Thus compare the opening words of *Mod. Ten. Cur.* p.1, with Jacob, *Ct.-Keeper* (1819), p.28.

But if this imposed a new uniformity on an important part of the manorial courts' business it did not affect the way that business was carried out and here, despite the standardising effect of the steward's manuals, there was a good deal of variety. Much of this variety arose from local customs, idiosyncratic ways of doing business on the particular manor. Since these affected only the method of reaching decisions they are unlikely to be mentioned on the formal record of the court's business, and we learn more of them through informal descriptions of proceedings by contemporaries. Thus we are told how on some Berkshire, Devon and Somerset manors in the seventeenth and eighteenth centuries a widow who had forfeited her right to her husband's copyhold by her unchastity could regain tenure by sitting astride a ram in the court, with her face to its tail, and while grasping its tail repeating a set formula.[17] Naturally, the more bizarre the custom, the more likely it is to have been recorded, and there must have been a great many minor details in which one manor's way of doing things differed from another's – differences which were quite insignificant but which were no doubt carefully remembered and as carefully observed in the particular court. But even in their formal proceedings and decisons, as recorded on their court rolls, we find considerable differences between one manor and another, and no great reluctance to depart from the detailed procedures recommended by the manuals.

However, the distinction between meetings of the court leet and of the court baron was usually carefully maintained; indeed, the court leet was sometimes specifically held in the name of the sovereign, unlike the court baron which was simply the court of the manorial lord. On the large manor of Wakefield court leets were held by themselves at three different centres in the seventeenth century, as well as combined with the court baron for the entire manor at Wakefield itself.[18] The most common arrangement however was for a court leet to be held at a single session with the court baron which also, as it usually met more often, will have been held on other occasions without the court leet; this is the pattern we find for instance at Lacock (Wiltshire) in the sixteenth and seventeenth centuries, at Hornsey (Middlesex) in the seventeenth, at Crondall (Hampshire) in the seventeenth and eighteenth.[19] Of course many manorial lords had no rights of court leet but, compared with medieval court rolls, a far larger proportion of surviving records seems to be of courts with both types of jurisdiction; perhaps those that had rights of court baron alone tended to disappear sooner – one of the many questions about post-medieval manorial courts to which we need the clear answer that only systematic research can give. But if the distinction between court baron and court leet was at least as clear as in the fourteenth and fifteenth centuries we must still be prepared for some variety of nomenclature. View of frankpledge (*visus franciplegii*) always implied a full session of court leet, but the exact meaning of such terms as great court, or genral court, or lawful court, or special court (*magna curia, curia generalis, curia legalis, curia specialis*) varied from one manor to another; at Wreyland (Devon) in the early eighteenth century the rolls for a court with some vestiges of leet jurisdiction call it simply 'a Court' in the headings.[20]

---

[17] G.L. Gomme, 'Widowhood in Manorial Law', *Archaeological Review*, ii (1889), pp.188–9; T. Blount, *Tenures of Land and Customs of Manors*, ed. W.C. Hazlitt (London, 1874), p.109.
[18] *Wakefield Ct. Rolls 1639–40*, pp.x, xvi.
[19] F.H. Hinton, 'Notes on the Court Books of the Manors of Lacock, Charlton, Liddington with Cote, and Nethermore (chiefly 1583 to 1603)', *Wiltshire Archaeological and Natural History Magazine*, l (1942–4), p.460; *Hornsey Ct. Rolls; Crondal Recs.* pp.488–96.
[20] *Wreyland Docs.* pp.xc–xciii, 73–88.

Occasionally a court was called a court of survey or court of recognition. This was a special meeting of a court baron, not a different kind of jurisdiction. A court of recognition would normally be the first meeting of the court after a new manorial lord had taken over, and its purpose was to get from the manor's tenants full details of their holdings and acknowledgement of the rents and services they owed; these would be recorded on the court roll. A court of survey would be a similar session, held whenever occasion required, to compile a formal survey of the manor, usually by one or more surveyors brought in for the occasion; usually they would just record the tenants' own statements of what they held and what they owed and would not make any inspection of the property, still less a measured survey.[21] In both sorts of court the tenants would be required to produce the deeds or copies of court roll by which they claimed tenure. There were medieval precedents for sessions of this kind; in the 1320s a Crowland Abbey court roll from Oakington (Cambridgeshire) in the first year of a new abbot had a note at the end 'to speak with the lord about the recognition of the villeins (de recognitione villanorum)', and one meeting of the court at Cuxham (Oxfordshire) was almost entirely devoted to compiling a manorial custumal.[22] However, they seem to have acquired formal status only in the sixteenth century, the period that saw the emergence in England of a distinct profession of surveyors. Even in the sixteenth century the difference between the court of recognition and the court of survey was often blurred, and by the nineteenth century the distinct court of recognition seems to have disappeared. A model for a court of survey then shows the steward himself inspecting the leases and copies brought to the court, making abstracts for entry on the court roll, and also drawing up a separate survey in tabular form, showing what each tenant held and on what terms, its annual value to the lord and the value of any heriots.[23] But some manorial surveys were much more elaborate; an early example is of Budbrooke (Warwickshire) in 1590, 'vewed and surveighed' by the steward and jury, a full terrier filling over 100 leaves of manuscript.[24] As evidence of who was holding lands within the manor even such detailed records can be misleading, notably in saying nothing of subtenancies.[25]

Another sort of session of the manorial court that we find certainly by the late seventeenth century was the private court baron. This was an ad hoc meeting of the court, with only a few suitors present, to transact a particularly urgent piece of business, a formalisation of what we saw happening in the middle ages when matters cropping up between infrequent meetings of a court were dealt with privately by the manorial lord.[26] But business might still be done wholly informally outside the manorial court. A writer in 1923 tells how 'I was present

---

[21] However, J. Norden, *The Surveyors Dialogue* (London, 1607; 2nd enlarged edn, London, 1610) gives the surveyor a larger role: he is to make a map of the manor, he takes a dominant part in the proceedings of the court of survey, even administering the tenants' oaths if licensed by the Crown to do so, and he offers the estate bailiff general advice on agricultural improvement.

[22] Page, *Crowland*, p.356; *Cuxham Man. Recs.* pp.656–61.

[23] Fisher, *Treatise*, pp.247–53, 275–7; Jacob, *Ct.-Keeper* (1819), pp.143–51, 336; cf. 23–7, 128–9.

[24] Warwick County Record Office, CR 895/80.

[25] E. Kerridge, *Agrarian Problems in the Sixteenth Century and After* (London, 1969), pp.48–53; C.J. Harrison, 'Elizabethan Village Surveys: a Comment', *Ag.H.R.* xxvii (1979), pp.82–9.

[26] *Crondal Recs.* p.490 (1685); Jacob, *Ct.-Keeper* (1713), pp.204–5; Fisher, *Treatise*, pp.224–32, describes special courts baron held for an admission under an enclosure act and for the admission of a bankrupt's assignees; J. Scriven, *A Practical Treatise on Copyhold Tenure and Court Keeping* (London, 1816), pp.6, 450, where private courts are said to be 'frequently held'.

once in the office of the Steward of the Manor of Newcastle-under-Lyme when a copyholder came to take his seisin. The particulars were entered, he was given his slip, and then the steward held out to him a rod, like a school-pointer, the end of which the claimant took in his hand for a moment, and the seisin was complete.'[27] By the nineteenth century very likely a great deal of business that properly belonged to the court baron was being transacted privately in the offices of solicitors or in estate-offices simply because the manorial court met so infrequently or not at all.

Besides the court leet and court baron there were two other kinds of private jurisdiction that in a few places survived from the middle ages. A very few honour courts continued in existence: the court of the honour of Clare (Suffolk), actually in royal hands, met throughout the eighteenth century.[28] And in quite a few places private rights of hundred jurisdiction were still exercised. There might be a regular hundred court, as for Bisley Hundred and the so-called Seven Hundreds of Cirencester (Gloucestershire), which continued to meet until 1792, dealing mostly with petty debts with a twice-yearly view of frankpledge.[29] Or the hundred court, if held at all, might be a purely formal occasion, the franchisal rights being exercised in the owner's local manorial courts, as probably happened in the dean and chapter of Winchester's hundreds of Elstob and Everleigh (Wiltshire) in the sixteenth and seventeenth centuries.[30] Or it might be entirely combined with a manorial court, like the hundred of Alton (Hampshire) in the early seventeenth century.[31] The 1819 edition of Jacob's *Complete Court-Keeper* still includes forms of procedure and model records for hundred courts held along with court leet and court baron.[32]

The frequency of meetings of manorial courts varied at least as much as in the middle ages. Some, like the court baron at Wakefield in the seventeenth century, met every three weeks. A court leet would not be held more than twice a year, and on some manors the court baron too would be held only on these two occasions, as at Lincoln Cathedral Close in the late seventeenth century.[33] But court leet and court baron might both meet less frequently still; thus at Fingringhoe (Essex) in the mid sixteenth century there was only one meeting a year for both types of jurisdiction, and at Wreyland (Devon) in the early eighteenth rather less.[34] The court baron at St Giles, Durham, was meeting about every seven years in the late nineteentth century.[35] Disuse did not extinguish the right to hold a court, so we sometimes find courts being revived after long intervals – at Leamington Spa (Warwickshire) in 1828 after a break of ninety years.[36] It follows that a long gap in a series of court records need not mean that

[27] C. Swynnerton, 'Some Early Court Rolls of the Manors of Stonehouse, King's Stanley, Woodchester, and Achards', *Transactions of the Bristol and Gloucestershire Archaeological Society*, xlv (1923), p.213.
[28] E. Margaret Thompson, *A Descriptive Catalogue of Manorial Rolls belonging to Sir H.F. Burke*, Manorial Soc. xi, xii (1922–3), ii, pp.13–14.
[29] *V.C.H. Gloucs.* xi, pp.2–3, 153; Webb, op. cit. i, p.60.
[30] *V.C.H. Wilts.* xi, p.107.
[31] Thompson, op. cit. ii, p.4; *V.C.H. Hants.* ii, p.471.
[32] Jacob, *Ct.-Keeper* (1819), pp.28–32, 59–62, 101–8, 111–18.
[33] C.L. Exley, 'The Leet or Manorial Court of the Cathedral Church of Lincoln', *The Lincolnshire Historian*, i (1947–53), pp.307–12.
[34] G. Benham, 'Manorial Rolls of Fingringhoe, West Mersea and Pete Hall, 1547 to 1558', *Essex Review*, l (1941), pp.189–90; *Wreyland Docs.* pp.lxxxix–xc.
[35] *Memorials of St. Giles's, Durham*, ed. J. Barmby, Surtees Soc., xcv (1896), pp.2–5.
[36] Webb, *Manor*, i, pp.18, 66n–67n.

any have been lost. Latterly the headings of court rolls often say where the court met – from 1757 onwards in the printed Wimbledon (Surrey) rolls for instance. Often, as at Wimbledon, this would be at an inn, though in many places there was a specific court-house or court-room even if seldom used for this purpose.

The official holding the courts was still the steward, though on large estates the office might be held by some important personage as an honorary dignity or sinecure, the actual work being done by a deputy; in any case a steward would often appoint a deputy to share the work and the court might be held by either of them. The basic procedure of the court, whatever the local variants, seems to have been everywhere the same as in the middle ages: juries would be chosen from among the court's suitors to answer questions put to them and to make presentments. It now came to be held, however, that where there was view of frankpledge there should be one body of jurors for the court leet, often called the jurors for the lord king (*juratores pro domino rege*), another, the homage (*homagium*), for the court baron – we find this in the seventeenth century at Hornsey (Middlesex) and at Stanton Lacy (Shropshire), where a clear distinction was maintained between the business of the two courts.[37] On some manors, however, a single jury served for both purposes – as at Tweedmouth (Northumberland), also in the seventeenth century, where no attempt was made to differentiate the business of court leet and court baron.[38] We occasionally find separate juries to make presentments and to give verdicts; this was the case at Bramhall (Cheshire) at the same period.[39] Transfer of copyhold tenements to or from the lord of the manor was normally effected by some simple ceremony: the touching of a stick held by the steward, as described at Newcastle-under-Lyme, is the exact ceremony specified by the printed treatise of 1510,[40] but as Sir Edward Coke wrote in the seventeenth century:

> In some Manors where a Copyholder surrendreth his Copyhold, he useth to hold a little rod in his hand, which he delivereth to the Steward or Bayliffe, according to the Custome of the Manor, to deliver it over to the party to whose use the Surrender was made in the name of Seisin, and from thence they are called Tenants by the Verge. In some Manors in stead of a wand a straw is used, and in other manors a glove is used, *Et consuetudo loci semper est observanda.*[41]

This dictum, 'The local custom must always be observed', is as basic to the manorial court in the nineteenth century as in the thirteenth, and it applies to the procedure as well as to the substantive local customs and by-laws. Thus although the manuals give us complete outlines of proceedings, we must expect to find many variations; some will appear in the court's formal records, others only in less formal descriptions. In some manors the regular business of the court included a perambulation of bounds – of the manor itself, as at St Giles, Durham, or of some particular piece of its property, as at Ermington (Devon), where the

---

[37] *Hornsey Ct. Rolls*; R.C. P[urton], 'A Manor Court at Stanton Lacy in 1609', *Transactions of the Shropshire Archaeological Society*, liii (1949–50), pp.207–11.

[38] Webb, *Manor*, i, p.95n.

[39] Webb, *Manor*, i, pp.91–3; H.W. Clemesha, 'The New Court Book of the Manor of Bramhall (1632–1657)', in *Chetham Miscellanies, New Ser. iv*, Chetham Soc. New Ser. lxxx (1921), pp.8–9.

[40] *Mod. Ten. Cur.* pp.25–6.

[41] Coke, *Copy-Holder*, p.104. B.L. Add. Charter 59780 shows seisin being given 'per stramen' to a copyholder at Laneham (Notts.) in 1699.

River Erme was perambulated as an assertion of fishing and pasture rights.[42] Much more commonly festivities of some sort, whether private or public, came to be a normal part of proceedings once the formal business was over.

The records of the court

Compiling the formal record of the court was the responsibility of the steward or deputy-steward who seems, more often than in, say, the fourteenth century, to have managed without a clerk's assistance at the actual session. The result was not always satisfactory: an early-eighteenth-century steward at Hitchin (Hertfordshire), according to his successor, 'made no rolls, nor hardly any copies, nor was capable of so doing, thereby introducing horrid Confusion in the affairs of the manor'.[43] The steward's custody of the records could also cause difficulties: the new manorial lord of Great Crawley (Buckinghamshire) in 1577 complained that his predecessor's steward was cutting up or defacing or giving away the many court rolls and rentals of the manor that he had in his possession.[44] At about the same period the bishop of London claimed that Hugh Stewkley, the former bishop's deputy-steward for several Middlesex manors, was improperly retaining their court rolls and other records, to which he replied that he had given some of the rolls to the bishop's officers and others, sealed in bags, to the reeves, farmers and churchwardens of the manors, as was customary there.[45] On the whole, manorial court records seem to have been carefully compiled and carefully preserved following the practice of the particular manor or estate.

However, Stewkley also said that he still had the notes from which the court rolls were written up. These were in paper books, along with similar notes from courts of other manors that no longer belonged to the bishopric. In point of fact the record made at the court itself seems now always to have been, at most, a rough draft of the court roll; from it the formal record of proceedings would be drawn up afterwards. It is not uncommon for these preliminary drafts or notes to survive; although by far the most usual surviving records of post-medieval manorial courts are the fair-copy court rolls, we have far more numerous and varied subsidiary records than those from the middle ages. The drafts written in court were normally on paper, sometimes in books – those for Crondall (Hampshire) in the seventeenth and eighteenth centuries are a surviving example – sometimes on sheets which might be formed into rolls, as at Wakefield in the seventeenth century.[46] Jacob's *Complete Court-Keeper*, in its successive editions from 1713 to 1819, calls the draft the minute-book of the court, and the instructions and forms for entries imply that it will approximate to a condensed version of the fair-copy court roll; when the steward has made the fair copy and has also made the appropriate copies of court roll for the copyholders he is told to put a line at the end of the draft and write 'Inrolled, and Copies made'.[47]

The finished court roll was typically a literal roll of parchment, as in the middle

[42] *Memorials of St. Giles's*, ed. Barmby, pp.5–8; 'First report of the Committee to obtain information as to the peculiar tenures of land and as to customs of manor courts, in Devonshire, exclusive of Dartmoor', *Report and Transactions of the Devonshire Association*, xii (1880), pp.155–7.

[43] R.L. Hine, *The History of Hitchin* (London, 2v., 1927–9), i, p.62.

[44] A.C. Chibnall, *Beyond Sherington* (London, 1979), p.35.

[45] *Hornsey Ct. Rolls*, pp.xvii–xviii.

[46] *Crondal Recs.* pp.488–96; *Wakefield Ct. Rolls 1639–40*, p.xxii.

[47] Jacob, *Ct.-Keeper* (1713), pp.64–70; (1819), pp.59–63; cf. Fisher, *Treatise*, p.236–46, 270–3.

ages (see Plate 8). Usually a roll would be for a single court, though several might be filed together to form a single exchequer-fashion roll, and sometimes, as in earlier periods, court followed court without starting a new membrane – as at Wreyland (Devon), where eighteen courts from 1696 to 1727 were enrolled on eleven membranes in all.[48] We have seen that on some medieval estates courts were entered in books instead of on rolls. This became a more common practice as time went on, though the date of the change varied greatly – at Ightham (Kent), for instance, in 1586 (interestingly the surviving rolls of 1553–74 were on paper) and at Wimbledon (Surrey) in 1726.[49] It need not follow that if the draft was written in a book the fair copy of the court roll would be too; at Crondall the drafts were in paper books but the fair copies were parchment rolls.[50] The published manuals on keeping manorial courts give specimens of court rolls for the various sorts of court as well as precedents for the many types of entry that might be found. In practice there was a good deal of variety, but in principle the form of the court roll followed medieval precedent and tradition and the actual order of business in the court: the heading was usually in standardised form with the name of the manor in the left margin, the essoins and list of jurors would be at the start of the roll, the names of the affeerors at the end. The manuals also give specimens of the copies of court roll that the steward would also make from his draft for the copyholders. Their form too followed earlier precedent: a heading like the court roll itself, with a note that the record of the court included the item that followed, and at the end the steward's signature and, sometimes, the seal of the lord of the manor. The copy of court roll was normally written on parchment, and copies were not restricted to the records of admissions but might be made for other entries touching the individual copyholder's rights, such as permission to sublet or a grant of the reversion of a holding.

In the mid sixteenth century the court roll would be written in Latin apart from statements of customs and by-laws and sometimes also individual ordinances which were normally in English.[51] From 1733 court rolls had to be in English, under the act of 1731 which said that English must be the language of all legal documents.[52] On some manors, as at Tweedmouth and Wimbledon, it was the act that produced the change of language, but on others it had occurred earlier – in 1708 at Ightham, for instance[53] – while everywhere court rolls were written in English during the 1650s under the Commonwealth.[54] Copies of court roll were written in the same language as the court roll itself, and so too usually was the draft. Other manorial court records were mostly in English, with the occasional phrase of legal Latin in some form or other – like the 'omney beney' (for omnia bene: all well) of one return of presentments made to the court at Wakefield in 1640.[55]

The fact that they are written in English is sometimes helpful in identifying estreat rolls; often their headings are much the same as those of the court rolls

---

[48] Wreyland Docs. p.73n.
[49] E. Harrison, op. cit. pp.183–4; Wimbledon Ct. Rolls, list of contents.
[50] Crondal Recs. pp.488–96.
[51] Thus Hinton, op. cit. pp.475–6 (manorial customs, 1586), Swynnerton, op. cit. p.211 (court order, 1589); an example of a by-law in Latin, 1552, is in Benham, op. cit., pp.199–200.
[52] 4 George II, c.26; the act came into operation on 25 March 1733.
[53] Webb, Manor, i, p.95n; Wimbledon Ct. Rolls; E. Harrison, op. cit. p.185.
[54] Under an act of 22 Nov.1650, annulled, as from 1 August 1660, by 12 Charles II, c.3.
[55] Wakefield Ct. Rolls 1639–40, pp.xxii, 156.

(occasionally, unhelpfully, specifically called 'Copy'), and some have been described in print as though they were the court rolls themselves.[56] In fact, of course, they simply list those entries from the court roll that gave rise to payments to be collected. The entries are generally much abridged, but the estreats may include information drawn from the detailed presentments that was omitted from the court roll. Thus comparing the estreats and the court roll for the bishop of London's manorial court at Hornsey on 26 April 1653, we find that the estreats list some forty defaulters, amerced 6d. each, who are not mentioned on the court roll; on the other hand, rearrangement of some entries has perverted their meaning, so it reads as if one man, amerced 'for the like offence' in both records, was being penalised for drunkenness whereas it was actually for illicitly taking bracken from the wood.[57]

The business of the court produced other records as well. Instructions for holding a court leet say that the tithingmen should hand the steward resient rolls, lists of those in the tithings; these would be read out in court for those present to answer their names, the lists being marked accordingly.[58] These are distinguished from the tenant list, apparently kept by the steward, who would mark on it the attendance at each court; Jacob's *Complete Court-Keeper* gives a specimen on which freeholders are marked L, copyholders C and leaseholders J, attendance at the court being shown as 'app.', essoin as 'ss.' and excused for age or illness as 'exc.'[59] In practice there was much variety and the exact status or purpose of existing lists of suitors can only be understood in the context of the particular manor and its other records. We find variety too in the way manorial orders and by-laws were recorded: often they were entered not (or not only) on the court roll itself but on a separate roll. This was the case in the late sixteenth century at Deddington (Oxfordshire) where in 1585 seven suitors formally complained that some recent orders had not been placed on the roll, and that in consequence 'we can not come to the sighte and viewe of them, as reason dothe allowe' – implying that the roll, or a copy of it, would be available locally for inspection.[60] Jacob's *Complete Court-Keeper*, in 1819 as in 1713, gives specimens of a roll of customs and a table of tenants' holdings and rents, both envisaged as being drawn up at a court of survey.[61] Another type of record described in Jacob's manual is the contract book, giving details of agreements made with prospective copyholders at one court for admission to their holdings at the next; the purchaser of the copyhold would sign the book and would himself be given a copy of the entry, signed by the steward.[62] At Wakefield in the seventeenth and eighteenth centuries so-called docket books were produced, listing (in Latin to 1707) the land transfers recorded on the court rolls, to which they served as an index.[63] The

[56] E.J.L. Cole, 'Kingsland – a Caroline Court Record, 1640', *Transactions of the Woolhope Naturalists' Field Club*, xxxvi (1958–60), pp.196–9; Exley, op. cit. pp.307–12.

[57] *Hornsey Ct. Rolls*, pp.117–20.

[58] Jacob, *Ct.-Keeper* (1819), pp.30–1; Webb, *Manor*, i, p.67.

[59] Jacob, *Ct.-Keeper* (1819), p.51; Fisher, *Treatise*, p.274, gives a similar form for what he calls a suit roll, attendance being shown by 'App.' or 'Ess.'

[60] H.M. Colvin, *A History of Deddington, Oxfordshire* (London, 1963), pp.69–70; at Chesham (Bucks.) in 1590 a manorial 'Customary Book' seems normally to have been kept by one of the tenants (*V.C.H. Bucks.* iii, p.209).

[61] Jacob, *Ct.-Keeper* (1713), pp.22–7, 486; (1819), pp.23–7, 336.

[62] Jacob, *Ct.-Keeper* (1713), pp.71–4; (1819), pp.64–7

[63] *Wakefield Ct. Rolls 1639–40*, p.x.

subsidiary records produced by the manorial court varied a good deal according to local circumstances and local practice.

Besides these ongoing records that were kept for reference, there were others made for a single session of a court. There would be the formal letter or precept from the steward to the local bailiff or other official ordering the court to be summoned, letters of attorney appointing proxies for particular items of business, warrants telling the local official to carry out orders of the court, and so on.[64] There would be the bills of charges for the court's expenses and for the fee of the steward or deputy-steward who held it.[65] Of these ephemeral records those that seem to survive most often are the bills of presentment: a small piece of paper or parchment handed in at the court by each of the local officials or juries with their presentments written out and attested by one or more signatures or marks. It is not clear whether these were normally drawn up in the court itself or prepared in advance – probably practice varied. They survive often because they were kept with the draft or minutes from which the court roll was ultimately drawn up, providing further information that might or might not be incorporated in the fair copy.[66] The seventeenth-century Wakefield court rolls include, with the draft rolls, particularly full and interesting files of these presentments. Among them are reports ('The stockes the whipp stockes the Buttes and the Pinfold and all other things in good repayre'), local orders ('Thomis Drake or the owners or ockopier of shibden mill to make A Sufficient bridge ouer against a place Called Damhead'), presentments of offenders ('George Feild for smiteing downe our Constable').[67] Here, as so often in manorial records of every period, we hear the authentic voice of the countryman breaking through the formalities of procedure and the technicalities of law and administration to find a place in the written record.

Select texts

Wimbledon Ct. Rolls. Court baron and court leet, 1462–1864. Only entries relating to common land and common rights, but these entries are numerous and varied. Latin text with translation to 1728; original English text from 1735.

Seven Somerton Court Rolls, ed. A. Ballard, Oxfordshire Archaeological Soc. Transactions, 50 (Banbury, 1906). Court baron and court leet, 1482–1573, including a court of survey, 1573. English translation.

R.C.P[urton], 'A Manor Court at Stanton Lacy in 1609', *Transactions of the Shropshire Archaeological Society*, liii (1949–50), pp.207–11. Court baron and court leet. English translation.

H.W. Clemesha, 'The New Court Book of the Manor of Bramhall (1632–1657)', in *Chetham Miscellanies, New. Ser. iv*, Chetham Soc. New Ser. lxxx (1921), pp.23–32. Court baron, 1632 and 1645, including lists of suitors. Mixed Latin and original English text.

[64] Thus Jacob, *Ct.-Keeper* (1819), pp.28–9, 43–5, 47–8, 50–1.
[65] e.g. the solicitors' accounts for holding the manorial court of Woodhouse (Leics.), 1826–9 (Leicestershire Record Office, DG9/1958).
[66] Webb, *Manor*, i, pp.39, 69, 88n.
[67] *Wakefield Ct. Rolls 1639–40*, pp.145, 101, 80.

Wakefield Ct. Rolls 1639–40. Court baron and court leet, with subsidiary documents. Abridged English translation, but with the full text of those subsidiary documents written in English.

C.L. Exley, 'The Leet or Manorial Court of the Cathedral Church of Lincoln', *The Lincolnshire Historian*, i, pt 8 (Autumn 1951), pp.309–12. Estreat rolls for the court held for Lincoln Cathedral Close, 1664–5. Original English text.

Wreyland Docs. pp.73–88. Court baron and court leet, 1696–1727. Original English text.

Further reading
There are general accounts of manorial courts and their work in the sixteenth century by E. Kerridge, *Agrarian Problems in the Sixteenth Century and After* (London, 1969), pp.17–31, and in 1689–1835 by Webb, *Manor*, i, pp.9–211. Hearnshaw, *Leet Jur.* is an invaluable and informative general survey, while concentrating particularly on court leets in boroughs and other towns. A very full, interesting account of the records and business of manorial courts in one county, 1558–1603, is provided by F.G. Emmison, *Elizabethan Life: Home, Work and Land* (Essex Record Office, Publication 69; Chelmsford, 1976), pp.197–333. The latest and by far the most comprehensive work on copyhold is C.I. Elton and H.J.H. Mackay, *A Treatise on the Law of Copyholds and Customary Tenures of Land* (London, 1893); of earlier treatises, Coke, *Copy-Holder*, is basic, being the source of much that appears in later works, and C. Watkins, *A Treatise on Copyholds* (London, 2v., 1797–9), is also important. The manuals for stewards holding manorial courts are textually very dependent one on another; Jacob, *Ct.-Keeper*, is probably the most often met with, and for this reason has been particularly referred to in this chapter, but there are many others (above, p.59n). T. Blount, *Tenures of Land and Customs of Manors*, ed. W.C. Hazlitt (London, 1874), is a miscellany of information, arranged alphabetically by places, about the way lands were held by lords and tenants; it includes many examples of post-medieval local manorial customs.

1. Custumal: Monxton (Hants.: Bec Abbey), *circa* 1230 with alterations mid 13th century. Muniments of King's College, Cambridge, Dd. 33. Printed in *Bec Docs.*, pp.46–7

    The custumal has been brought up to date by crossing out or erasing the names of former tenants and entering the new ones.

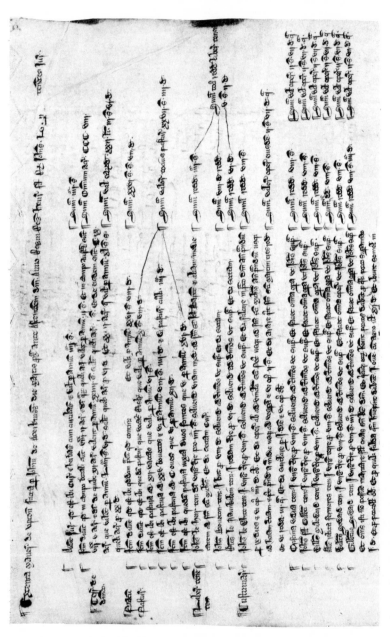

2. Extent: Upton (Berks.: Adam de Stratton), 1271. P.R.O. SC11/713. Printed in *Stratton Accts.*, pp.17–19

The demesne is described in summary form, but in the standard order of the extent: manor-house, arable, meadow, pasture. There follow the free and customary tenants with their rents and services. Total areas, rents and valuations are entered on the right.

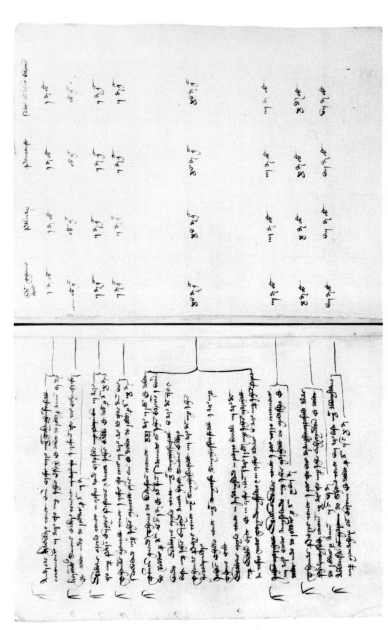

3. Rental: Wye (Kent: crown estates), 1452–4. P.R.O. E315/433, ff.85v–86r. Printed in *A Survey of the Manor of Wye*, ed. Helen E.Muhlfeld (New York, 1933), pp.140–3

The rents due from each holding are entered on the right-hand page under the four days when they were due: the feast of St Thomas the Apostle (21 December), Palm Sunday, Whitsun and the Nativity of St John Baptist (24 June).

4. Phase 1 account: Itchingswell (Hants.: bishop of Winchester), 1210–11. Hampshire Record Office, Eccl.2/159270B. Printed in *Winch.*
Pipe Roll 1210–11, pp.104–6

This is entered on a roll of the year's accounts for all the bishop of Winchester's manors; above is the end of the account for Ashmansworth and below is the start of the account for Fareham (both Hants.), all obvious fair copies and written at a single operation.

5. Phase 2 account: Cuxham (Oxon.: Merton College), 1348–9. Muniments of Merton College, Oxford, 5875, m.2. Printed in *Cuxham Man. Recs.*, pp.449–50

The end of the cash charge account and the start of the cash discharge. Some totals and the whole of the 'Sales at the audit' paragraph have been added at the audit by the auditor's clerk; the difference in handwriting is clear.

74

6. Phase 3 account: Bishop's Clyst (Devon: bishop of Exeter), 1428–9. Devon Record Office, W.1258.G.3(4). Printed in N.W.Alcock, 'An East Devon Manor in the Later Middle Ages', *Report and Transactions of the Devonshire Association*, cv (1973), p.182
    The end of the cash discharge account, with its total and balance on a separate membrane, formerly sewn on but now detached. As usual, in the notes following the balance (here notes of payments) each successive line starts further to the left.

7. Medieval court roll: Oakington, with Cottenham and Dry Drayton (Cambs.: Crowland Abbey), 1291. Muniments of Queens' College, Cambridge. Printed in Page, *Crowland*, pp.333–5

Payments imposed are entered in the left margin, with a note of the manor to which each entry refers.

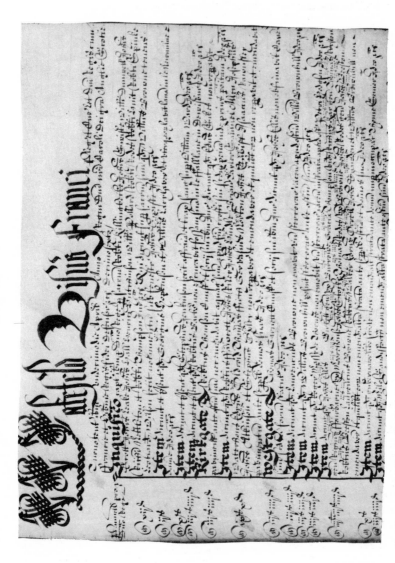

8. Post-medieval court roll: Wakefield (W. R. Yorks.: Sir Gervase Clifton), 1640. Yorkshire Archaeological Society, MD225/1/365. Printed in *Wakefield Ct. Rolls 1639–40*, pp. 119–20

An obvious fair copy written up after the court had ended. Payments imposed are entered in the left margin; some of these are totals, the individual amounts being entered above the names in the text.

INDEX

Manorial records

before

P D A Harvey

Professor of Mediaeval History
in the University of Durham

British Records Association

Archives and the User   *No 5*

1984

ISBN : 0 900222 06 9
©British Records Association, 1984
© British Records Association, 1984

Produced for the Association by
Alan Sutton Publishing, Gloucester
Printed in Great Britain by
Redwood Burn Limited Trowbridge